The Encyclopedia of

Professional Wrestling

100 Years of the Good, the Bad and the Unforgettable

Kristian Pope & Ray Whebbe Jr.

Published by

 **krause
publications**

700 East State Street • Iola, WI 54990-0001
715/445-2214 • FAX: 715/445-4087   www.krause.com

Please call or write for our free catalog of publications. Our toll-free number to place an order or
obtain a free catalog is 800-258-0929 or please use our regular business telephone 715-445-2214.

Library of Congress Catalog Number 20-01086363
ISBN 0-87349-233-1

Acknowledgments

For those of you who read our first book, *Professional Wrestling Collectibles*, we say thank you for stopping by again. For our new readers, we would like to extend a warm welcome.

In this book, *The Encyclopedia of Wrestling: 100 Years of the Good, the Bad and the Unforgettable*, we try again to reveal some of the incredible history of professional wrestling and great wrestling collectibles. Here, new fans to wrestling will find an entry point into the rich history of the sport, while true-blue fans will get a refresher course in the last 100 years which have shaped that strange but fascinating world of pro wrestling.

Part of the challenge in putting a wrestling history book together is in answering one question: Where do you start? That is something that drove the both of us crazy at times. Truly, the entire, unabridged history of pro wrestling is so incredibly extensive that no book could ever do it justice. Upon closer examination of wrestling, every year has new twists and turns and changes that could warrant a reference all their own.

What you will find here is a trip down memory lane. You will read about names you know and some names that—while they are indeed old—are seemingly made new again.

Of course, we like to think that the incredible black-and-white photographs that are courtesy of wrestling historian Norman Kietzer's archives tell a story all on their own. If you look closely, the pictures in this book will say more about wrestling history than any words we could conjure.

Spread throughout the book are samples of different wrestling memorabilia that have been found over the years. In a way, the collectibles tell stories as well about where the sport came from, where it is, and where it will go from here.

The support we have received as a result of our first effort has been tremendous. A sincere and heartfelt thanks goes to everyone that cared to read our work, those who wrote letters of encouragement, and those who simply browsed at the local book store.

Several people were integral in making this project work. Without them, our efforts would have failed. The greatest aspect of wrestling is the fans and the friends that we all meet as a result of our common bond. That closeness has been galvanized during this process and has regenerated our enthusiasm for giving back to the fans in the form of this book.

So thank you to Norm and Dr. Mike Lano. Without the use of their pictures and insights, you would not have this book in your hands. Thank you to Kris Manty and Paul Kennedy at Krause Publications for their incredible guidance, support, and friendship. We'd also like to send our appreciation to: Pat Hollis, Eddie Sharkey, Mick Karch, Dave Meltzer and the *Wrestling Observer Newsletter*, Terry Katzman at Garage D'Or Records in Minneapolis, Royal Duncan, General Adnan Al-Kaissey, Bruce Hart, Derrick Dukes, Ricky Rice, Fancy Ray McCloney, Dr. Greg Olson, West Potter, Scott McLin, Jim Valley, Alex Marvez, Tadd Kozeniewski, Dr. Bob Bryla, and Azteca Records.

Most importantly, we would like to thank our families. To Samantha Emilife, Ida Whebbe and the Pope family, your love and support has meant everything to us.

So there you have it. We can only hope you enjoy reading this book as much as we enjoyed writing it. Of course, we love hearing from wrestling fans, just like us, from all over the world. If you have any comments, questions, complaints, or corrections, send them via e-mail to kristianpope@earthlink.net.

Until next time, here comes the good, the bad, and the unforgettable.

Kristian Pope and Ray Whebbe Jr.

INTRODUCTION

One-hundred years of professional wrestling. The mere thought of that can leave a writer as drowsy as a fallen wrestler after a sleeper hold.

The thought of chronicling 100 years of anything, let alone wrestling, poses serious questions: What is professional wrestling? Is it a sport or form of entertainment? Who watches wrestling and why? How does the history of wrestling affect the product we see today on television? Is there a way to connect all the dots?

In this book, we will try to answer some of those questions by looking at where wrestling started and where it is today. To be certain, a look at 100 years in the history of frying pans would show numerous trends and changes. To tackle this wonderful world of professional wrestling will be our task. Those of you who enjoyed *Professional Wrestling Collectibles* will know that the collectibles phenomenon associated with wrestling is another fascinating aspect to the sport's history. Therefore, the book will also offer a glimpse into the pieces of memorabilia that help chronicle the past century in the ring.

Because wrestling is fairly subjective and regional, a fan growing up in Omaha, Nebraska will have different beliefs, likes, and dislikes than that of a fan from Tokyo, Japan. But one common thread binds all of us: As wrestling fans, wrestling has touched our nerves and our hearts and all for different reasons. Those who will share wresting experiences with us through this book will certainly come from different walks of life, but we all are alike in our desire to witness the sport's amazing display of athletic feats and entertaining appeal. We may be attracted to professional wrestling for different reasons, but we are all in agreement that there is no greater show on earth.

Through the use of photographs from wrestling historian Norman Kietzer's library, different tales of the sport can be told. Be it Antonino Rocca throwing his amazing bare-footed drop kick or a poster hyping a big card at a local arena, the true story of fans' appeal to wrestling can be explained. Photographs allow us to be up close and personal to the stars and feel the magnitude of importance of the event taking place and its relevance to the history and evolution of the sport.

One-hundred years of professional wrestling: From "shoots" to "works," Carneys to Crushers, heroes to villains, it's all here in a bold and colorful manner which only the grand scale world of professional wrestling would dare to reveal.

Contents

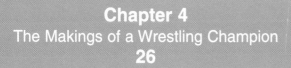

Chapter 1

Why We Are All Fans

"To those who believe in the beauty of professional wrestling, nothing needs to be said. For those who don't appreciate wrestling, nothing could be said to change their minds." —Vincent K. McMahon Jr., owner of the World Wrestling Federation.

"Professional wrestling is the oldest sport in the world. Native Americans have been grappling for thousands of years." —Clyde Bellecourt, co-founder of the American Indian Movement.

"While at times it seems to be a trend-setter, throughout history, whatever is going on in society in any part of the world is what we see in a wrestling ring. For the most part, wrestling mirrors society and gives people a much-needed outlet." —Bruce Hart, promoter and retired wrestler from the Calgary Stampede promotion.

"Is it real or isn't it? What is tough and does it really matter? Wrestling is about giving fans a product they love and will pay to see." —Norman Kietzer, six-decade wrestling journalist and historian.

The four quotes above come from men who will probably never be together in one room. Yet, everything that could be said to explain this sport can be summed up in their quotes. Like anything else, wrestling has made numerous changes over the past 100 years. For that matter, it has probably changed over the last 100 days. Watch a pay-per-view put together by the World Wrestling Federation and we might see the face of wrestling change over the following 100 minutes.

The great 1970s rock band Led Zeppelin, which happens to be one of wrestling-turned-Governor of Minnesota Jesse Ventura's favorite groups, once sang, "The song remains the same." To wrestling, that song is appropriately titled.

World Wrestling Federation fans show their passion for various grapplers, including The Rock.

Despite computer-generated graphics, mainstream publicity, pyrotechnic tricks, and slick television production, at its core, pro wrestling really has not changed all that much over 100 years. There are still heroes and villains, winners and losers, franchise players and underdogs, and fans with an insatiable desire to include wrestling in their lives in some shape or form.

From the closet fan to the impassioned collector, we all share a love for the sport. At times, we're fans whose eyes gaze in wonderment at the spectacle. At other times, we're cheerleaders. Who can't be effected by the raw, unbridled charisma of the performers? At other times still, we're critics. We get mad at storylines and finishes that make no sense or at gimmicks that rub us the wrong way. It's all part of being a fan.

Little has been published about wrestling, even though the sport totally embarrasses Major League Baseball in television viewers.

Gorgeous script for a gorgeous performer

Everything Gorgeous George did was extravagant. His robes were colored purple and red and were known to have lace and chiffon decorating them. George used to spend hours every day while on his wrestling tour's visiting local beauty shops and posing for the press. It is said that George also rode to the arenas in an orchid-colored Cadillac limousine. Like any piece of his memorabilia, Gorgeous George autographs are a difficult find. When George did take time to sign an autograph, however, he always wrote this passage: "Gorgeously yours, Gorgeous George." North Carolina wrestling fan West Potter found this George autograph and accompanying Georgie Pin through an Internet auction site. Potter won't be selling his Gorgeous George memorabilia anytime soon. "They are our links to the history of wrestling," Potter said. George would be thankful for that.

But in one year, more books are seemingly written about the "nations' pastime" than have been written about the "king of sports" over the previous 100 years.

"Promoters always felt snubbed by the media and press, so in turn they were protective of the business," says longtime Minneapolis fan Pat Hollis. "The only thing the media seems to want to do is take pot-shots at wrestling and call it fake."

The notion of "exposing the business" was probably the biggest mortal sin a wrestler could do. Only a chosen few were allowed to be part of the fraternity and that privilege

Vince McMahon is the most profitable wrestling promoter of all time.

Even Elvis Presley was a wrestling fan. Here he discusses some business with Whipper Billy Watson.

came only after a process of paying dues and a so-called promoters' security check that would make the KGB at its prime extremely proud.

That one word, "fake," has been known to get more than a few involved in wrestling upset with the press. In 1986, America's most famous wrestling hero, Hulk Hogan, nearly choked Richard Belzer into oblivion for saying the "F" word. Hogan's WWF pal, David Schultz, cracked ABC reporter John Stossel upside the head so hard during a wrestling exposé that Stossel was left with permanent ear damage.

Being part of the media covering professional wrestling an be a serious hazard to one's well-bring. That fact, combined with book publishers' notorious and comical belief that wrestling fans don't read, can help explain why so few books about the sport of kings have been written.

Tape trading, fans who bonded through the mail (and now through the Internet), and promoters changed all that. Prior to 1985, any information given about a wrestler was standard drivel. By the 1980s, the "F" word (fake) was nonexistent. But for many fans, that thirst for information was a driving force in their lives. For most of modern-day wrestling's history, fans and the sport were shunned. Those who enjoyed the sport hid in the closet and would meet secretly on ballfields, basement and backyard rings, and at wrestling parties. Every neighborhood had them, but the detractors were plenty.

From the 1940s through the 1980s—and to a certain extent, today—when a wrestler succeeded in mainstream acceptance, we all

Morales, a star for the masses

Fan clubs have a long history in pro wrestling. During the 1960s and 1970s, it was common for nearly every major name in the sport to have a fan club—and they were just that. The folks who ran the clubs were just ordinary fans with an extraordinary passion for a particular wrestler. Typically, fan clubs were established for "good guys." During the 1970s, one of the more well-known good guys was Pedro Morales. He excited crowds up and down the East Coast and in the World Wrestling Federation. Clubs would send out monthly or annual newsletters which tracked a wrestler's exploits around the country. Before cable TV and the Internet, one of the only ways to stay up to date with your favorite wrestler was through a network of pen pals and fan clubs. This button, worth around $15, was given out to members of Morales' club members. Today, fan clubs are seen in another form: Web sites.

Seasoned grapplers are often the idols of today's wrestlers. Here, six-time world champ and legend Lou Thesz pals with WWF champ Kurt Angle.

shared in the glory. If an Associated Press photo of a wrestler made it into the daily newspapers, we all cheered. When a wrestler was seen on a television show or in a film, we all watched. When mainstream society began to jump on the popularity of wrestling and ride its coattails to profit, we all wondered, "What took so long?"

A lot has changed. Today, wrestlers are everywhere. The Rock sat next to President George W. Bush at the Republican

Convention last year. Chyna was a Playboy magazine cover model and has been on numerous television shows. Jay Leno of the "Tonight Show" even entered the ring to beat World Championship Wrestling's Eric Bischoff. The WWF has earned gold records with music discs. "Entertainment Tonight," Craig Kilborn's "Late, Late Show," "That '70s Show," Howard Stern, "Saturday Night Live," and hundreds of other shows have all utilized wrestlers as of late in one way or another.

It may seem to be a modern-day spectacle now, but wrestling has always been imbedded in pop culture despite the media snub. In Mexico, El Santo and the Blue Demon made more than 100 movies between them and reached god-like status amongst the public. East Coast legend Antonino Rocca cut an album in the 1950s.

Fans love Rob Van Dam.

Minneapolis' Verne Gagne hawked vitamins in the 1960s. In Japan, the popular Tiger Mask wrestler is a character derived from a children's cartoon program. You name it—when it comes to professional wrestlers, they truly have been there, done that.

Whatever your background, wrestling has made its impact on the soul. The young watch with hypnotic-like wonderment and older people watch it with child-like faith. In Japan, many high-society members grab the first-row seats, similar to the chosen few who are invited to the opening of a Broadway play. There are no stereotypical wrestling fans. The link between all of us lies in the passion. For some, being a fan is enough. However, there are those daring few who are truly bitten by the wrestling bug. These folks become collectors, writers, promoters, referees, photographers, announcers, part of the ring crew, or webmasters. A few even don the tights and become wrestlers themselves.

Finishing moves like Karl Gotch's famed atomic-suplex hold keep fans coming back for more.

At one time, magazines gave a look into the wackiness in other wrestling worlds. In the 1950s, youths could only wonder if all Mongolians did have big muscles and odd haircuts. Did Sicilians look like Tony Altamore and Captain Lou Albano? What kind of match would the WWF champion Bruno Sammartino have against the NWA champion Terry Funk or Lou Thesz? Prior to videotapes, the only place to get information about other wrestling leagues, besides the one seen locally, was through magazines. For some unknown reason, magazines covered up real names and backgrounds and made up things they thought promoters and fans wanted to hear. Nobody was to be let in on the secrets.

But that mystery is what draws us in. Any living, breathing fan knew that Bruiser Brody

A lot of the ring action is pre-rehearsed, but the pain on Buh Buh Dudley's face looks all too real, as he gets smashed by Balls Mahoney and Musato Tanaka.

Bruiser Brody gets the upper hand on Harley Race.

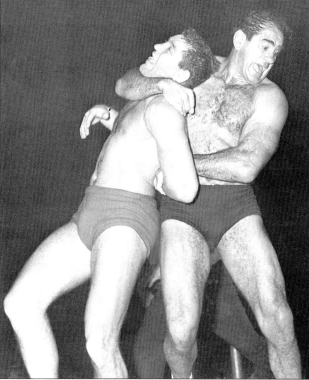

During a champion match on Jan. 28, 1964, Lou Thesz retains his heavyweight title against Danny Hodge when, after taking a fall each, both wrestlers were unable to continue.

could beat a wimpy foe like Greg Gagne into a bloody pulp. Few deep down believed Bob Backlund could really hold back monsters from eerie places found by Lou Albano, the Grand Wizard, and Fred Blassie. Most knew deep down that the Road Warriors and

Abdullah the Butcher were fellow human beings, but none of us could really believe we would see them at our local PTA meeting. Perhaps that was, and still is, the beauty of wrestling.

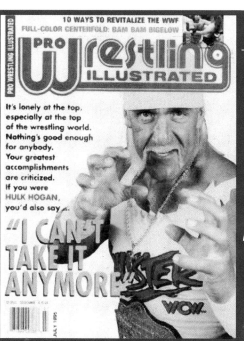

Fans can't get enough of Hogan's mug

For five decades, Pro Wrestling Illustrated has been synonymous with professional wrestling. Before the days of revealing the insider secrets of wrestling, the magazine was looked upon as the No. 1 journal of the sport. Under the leadership of former editor Bill Apter, promotions all around the world respected PWI. The editors, naturally, were fans of wrestling and tried their best to help move storylines forward. With the advent of insider newsletters and the Internet, there are hardly any secrets anymore. But PWI has stuck to its guns and prefers to write wrestling stories that presume the matches and television developments are real. While old magazines are not as popular in wrestling collecting as other sports, old issues of PWI are indeed bought, sold, and traded. Early issues can be found for under $50 and newer issues, such as this one, will be found for $10.

Chapter 2

Roots of the Ring

Wrestling's roots can be traced to the Biblical days. Every part of the entire world embraced and participated in the sport, in one way or another. Native Americans grappled throughout the mainland for thousands of years. The early Greeks grappled and contested in feats of strength in historic coliseums before thousands of spectators.

In fact, the Greek style was very rugged, based on rules that could be compared with today's ultimate fighting and mixed martial arts. The Greeks called their wrestling "pancration." Thousands of years later, in the 1990s, a group of worldwide warriors and Japanese business leaders call their promotion "Pancrase" in honor of the Greek battle mongers. The Greeks had a champion named the Mighty Milo, who was often imitated as a wrestling gimmick in the 1940s and 1950s. He was said to be so powerful, he trained for his contests by lifting cattle.

Because world news carried slowly until modern times,

wrestling history is very sketchy until the 1800s. The Roman Empire was noted for its impressive grapplers and strongmen. As the Olympics evolved, the Greco-Roman style was honored. Europeans and the British immigrated to the United States in the 1700s and by the 1800s, a myriad of wrestling styles existed in America. When soldiers entertained each other by grappling during the Civil War, those in attendance were treated with a very eclectic sporting contest. Carnivals and traveling entertainment troupes honed in on America's love of strength and combat. From pre-Civil War times to the late 1950s, carnivals loved to "work" crowds with wrestling. Hometown strongmen would bet hard-earned pay to beat the carnival champion, who often showed vulnerability in a faked match with a touring pal. The carnies, who were the promoters and managers, would milk the scenario for side bets, admission fees, and occasionally "mark" a cash prize if

Stanislaus Zbyszko gets ready to take on the Great Gama in India. Born in Poland, Zbyszko was a world champion from the 1920s, is said to be the first wrestler billed as the "8th Wonder of the World," and was also the first wrestler to earn $1 million. He was also a World War II Allied translator.

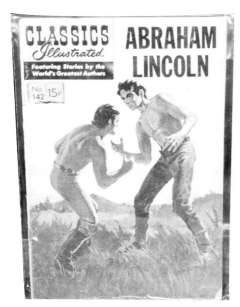

Abe Lincoln comic, $45. Photo courtesy of Mike Chapman.

they could defeat, or even last, just 10 minutes with the carnie pro. Needless to say, few regular folk were up to the task.

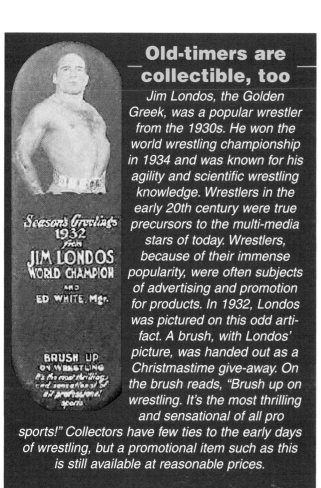

Old-timers are collectible, too

Jim Londos, the Golden Greek, was a popular wrestler from the 1930s. He won the world wrestling championship in 1934 and was known for his agility and scientific wrestling knowledge. Wrestlers in the early 20th century were true precursors to the multi-media stars of today. Wrestlers, because of their immense popularity, were often subjects of advertising and promotion for products. In 1932, Londos was pictured on this odd artifact. A brush, with Londos' picture, was handed out as a Christmastime give-away. On the brush reads, "Brush up on wrestling. It's the most thrilling and sensational of all pro sports!" Collectors have few ties to the early days of wrestling, but a promotional item such as this is still available at reasonable prices.

The ascension of Honest Abe

Prior to the Civil War, a tall, lanky genius, Abraham Lincoln, was making a pretty fair name for himself as a wrestler. His exploits were often covered in local newspapers, as radio, television and computers were something left only to the imagination during the 1850s.

Honest Abe, as he was nicknamed, won his first United States championship in 1931 at the age of 21 by beating Jack Armstrong. No less than a dozen "Armstrongs" carried on Jack's namesake in later years.

Lincoln certainly was the precursor to Jesse Ventura by catapulting wrestling to the elected office, yet because of his profound public deeds, his stand on slavery and subsequent brutal death, it was not until recently that the public realized the glory of Abe's grappling success. The International Wrestling Institute and Museum in Newton, Iowa has dedicated an entire exhibit to Lincoln.

Muldoon becomes an icon

By the later 1880s, inklings of true professional wrestlers were popping up in most communities. Saloon frequenters and ship workers were recipients of some early battles that were known to last as long as eight to ten hours. The first mega-star may have been William Muldoon. Muldoon was probably the sport's first pure professional and a superstar known throughout the land. After the war, the Union front-line soldier, drummer, and wrestler joined the rugged New York Police Department. To keep his grappling skills harp on weekends, he would lease his services to the highest-bidding tavern proprietor and would take on all comers. In 1887, Muldoon was featured on one of the first trading cards ever made. The Allen and Ginters endorsement may have been one of the first recorded deals of that kind.

Muldoon's first championship came earlier in 1883 by defeating Eddie Bibby in another

Gotch stands tall, even 75 years later

Frank Gotch is widely considered the finest technical wrestler the world has ever seen. The Humboldt, Iowa native was a traveling fighter in the early 1900s and is remembered as the "real" world champion. Gotch's private collection is on display at the International Wrestling Institute and Museum in Iowa. Museum curator and author Mike Chapman has displayed various artifacts of Gotch's, such as his wrestling gear, personal affects, and a trunk the wrestler used when traveling. This reproduction of a Police Gazette magazine cover featuring Gotch from 1916 is one of the items found at the museum. Gotch died at the young age of 39 of uremia poisoning, but his legend lives on at the Iowa wrestling museum.

Farmer Burns opens the door

Martin "Farmer" Burns had few equals when it came to ring generalship and technique. He was fast, well conditioned and deserving of recognition along with the celebrated William Muldoon as one of the greats. With Muldoon gallivanting around the world with John L. Sullivan, Burns was one of many recognized by promoters as a champion. There were no wrestling tabloids at the time and news of the sport seemed to move slow. Cannon, Jenkins and Burns were the top grapplers, with Burns being the easiest sell, even though some folks had difficulty knighting a man named "farmer." Burns was recognized by most to be champ, but in Iowa, he found a young ex-high school jock to have even more talent than Burns possessed.

While barnstorming through Iowa, the wise Farmer watched in awe as a small-town lad tossed champions around the little carnie ring like rag dolls. Burns, already tiring of living in Muldoon's shadows, knew this youngster had the goods to go far and signed him to a managerial contract. Burns was sure he could make this Iowan the best in the world. That young man just so happened to be Frank Gotch, who may have been the most unbeatable ring warrior in history. It took awhile, but after three years of intense training, the two began campaigning in Alaska. In storybook fashion, they mined for gold in the day and wrestled the laborers for their pay in the evening.

storied bay front city, San Francisco. He was now truly the sport's first traveling champion. Eventually, news of Muldoon's exploits were heard globally. Japan's Great Sorakichi, Scotland's Donald Dinne, and England's Tom Cannon ventured to the States in hopes of winning Muldoon's gold, but went home empty-handed.

Only German strongman Carl Abs and the first Dr. Bill Miller held the illustrious champion to a draw. His match with Miller reportedly lasted nearly 10 hours. Muldoon retired from championship competition in 1892 undefeated. He donned as the next champion, the little known Ernie Rober, who was worthy of the title but never grabbed America's hearts. Following a true-life hero like Muldoon would be an insurmountable task. Prior to retiring, an alliance with boxing champion John L. Sullivan proved to be Muldoon's greatest career move. It allowed him to quit dodging bullets in the streets of New York and the two legitimized both sports. Their touring troupe took rings sports out of saloons and farmlands and brought them into the mainstream.

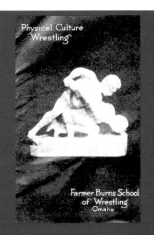

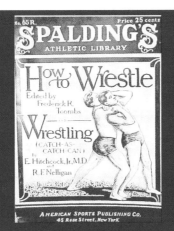

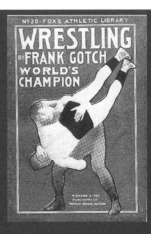

Classic lessons from some classic American wrestlers

Wrestling merchandise that pre-dates the Golden Age is hard to come by. Historical references of men like Frank Gotch and Farmer Burns (Gotch's trainer and mentor) are mainly limited to the printed word. Newspaper articles are one place to find the history, as are books like these. All three books were released in the mid-1910s. Gotch wrote "Wrestling" in 1913 and it was published by the Fox Athletic Library. Another book called "How to Wrestle" was released in 1915. And Burns' school of wrestling compiled a title called the "Physical Culture of Wrestling." All three books deal with real mat wrestling, what would be called "shoot" wrestling today. Submission holds were mainstays in this era. Sometimes matches lasted for hours at a time. The books offer a rare glimpse into a time when wrestling was considered the sport for tough men only.

In August 1901, Gotch earned a then-record purse of $10,000 by embarrassing Silas Archer for the Yukon Gold title. The match lasted nearly 20 minutes and was so gripping, miners threw nearly $9,000 in gold nuggets into the ring to honor the champ who had become accepted as one of their own. Grapplers throughout the world continued to lay claim to championships, but most of them refused to enter the same state, let alone ring, as the Iowa powerhouse. In 1904, with championship claimants plentiful, dozens of top-flight sports promoters banded together to form the National Wrestling Alliance. With one champion for the Alliance, promoters believed they would be able to keep the sport productive, vital, and true. The majority of the time's sportswriters agreed.

On May 4, 1904, longtime champion claimant and Muldoon nemesis geared up to prove their superiority by facing Europe's sensation George Hackenschmidt in New York City for the NWA world championship. More than 100 members of the media were in attendance. The suit, tie, and top-hat crowd was bountiful and smoke filled the air

as Hackenschmidt prevailed over the recognized North American champion, Jenkins. At this point in time, boxing and wrestling were the only two sports to have truly recognized world competition. Wrestling even earned more respect than its fistic kin because many states and countries deemed the sport illegal and even more countries had no serious heavyweight contenders. Hackenschmidt, also dubbed the Russian Lion, defended the belt and his usual European belts for nearly four years nobly.

Original photos of George Hackenschmidt, $35. Photo courtesy of Mike Chapman.

The champ was a man who seemed to want no part of Farmer Burns' charge, Gotch.

Gotch took advantage of his once-in-a-lifetime opportunity to face Hacksenschmidt on April 3, 1908 before 30,000 frenzied spectators in Chicago. He defeated the Russian Lion two falls straight. Gotch first pinned Hackenschmidt in the first fall. After absorbing two hours of punishment to his body, Hackenschmidt wearily conceded the second fall to Gotch. Up to that date, it was the largest paid gate in United States wrestling history. Hackenschmidt may deserve his spot among the greats, but after the war he had that night in the Windy City, athletically the Russian Lion was never the same.

Life was good for Gotch as a champion. He opened several Iowa-based businesses, picked up numerous endorsement deals, wed Gladys Oestrich in 1911, and toured the word before standing-room-only crowds with a theatrical play about his life winning the gold title. Burns, meanwhile, never appreciated Hackenschmidt for dodging Gotch in the first place. Burns and Gotch made Hackenschmidt wait three years for a rematch in which Gotch punished the Russian Lion severely during two straight fall victories before a crowd of 55,000 at Comiskey Park in Chicago—oddly enough, the same city in which Gotch had originally cornered the German heavyweight.

Gotch was a fighting champion who respected global forces. He held back German Jess Westerguard, the Middle East's Mahout Yussif and other top-rated foes throughout the world. Charlie Cutler, who seemed to be everyone's favorite top contender, gave a good outing against Gotch, but over a five-year span, the expert at submission holds retired as an undefeated champion. His last defense was against George Lurich on April 1, 1913. Sadly,

several years after walking away a winner, Gotch died of kidney failure at the age of 35. Doctors, knowing Gotch lived a clean life, linked the breakdown of his damaged liver to the severe pounding he took while training under Burns and from his 15 years of ring wars.

The Gotch-Hackenschmidt I clash was to that era what Joe Frazier-Muhammed Ali was 60 years later. Films of the historic match-up were sold to movie houses around the world. The match may have taken years to make, but the two must have appreciated the wait—after the Gotch-Hackenschmidt picture company out of Chicago sold state's rights to own the film. The two certainly knew how to sell a fight. Advertisements released by the film company asked, "Was Hackenschmidt yellow?" and "Did the Russian lay down?" Though the wars that Gotch had in the ring were far different by today's standards, make no mistake: No matter how powerful and talented today's wrestlers are, Frank Gotch was, above all, a professional wrestler.

He'd tie your legs in a knot and smile

Some the oldest collectibles from the early 20th Century that fans have are photographs. This 1930s photo postcard of former world champion Joe Stecher demonstrating a leg grapevine on a hapless foe, is a piece that harkens back to a time when wrestling was a struggle of athletic prowess. Postcards such as this are rare. Today, avid collectors say early century photos like this can be found for as high as $100, depending on quality. Stecher, in his prime, was known as a master technician. Because he was such a monumental figure in wrestling, the value of his old artifacts are high.

Chapter 3

The Belts: Wrestling's Main Organizations Crown Their Champions and Mold the 1900s

Bruno Sammartino, one of wrestling's all-time greats, was a true gentleman in and out of the ring and set the bar for champions. In his heyday, he regularly sold out Madison Square Garden.

Most of wrestling's history, prestige, and honor comes from the history of the world championship. For the better part of the 1900s, one organization, the national Wrestling Alliance (NWA), was the premiere organizing body for professional wrestling. Toward the tail end of the 1900s, other organizations like the American Wrestling Association (AWA) and the World Wrestling Federation (WWF) crowned their own champions. But before there was Vince McMahon Jr. and Ted Turner, only the NWA-sanctioned title had any worth in North America.

In the last century, the NWA crowned many champions. But within all of those title changes, wrestling historians can track important trends in the sport. More importantly, the early 1900s were essentially the years where professional wrestling as we know it began. A big reason for that was the NWA.

The NWA harkens the days of the early twentieth century. The NWA recognized the current champion and tried to make sense out of the disorder that was wrestling during the early 1900s. At the time, numerous men claimed to be the holders of the United States title, and others the National title. The title of wrestling champion went back and forth between numerous stars of the past and often via controversial terms. Until around 1930, the early foundation of wrestling was being laid.

George Hackenschmidt defeated Tom Jenkins in New York in 1904 to win one title. Frank Gotch then went on to defeat "Hack" four years later to become the undisputed champion. Others may have laid claim to a belt, but few wanted to get into a shoot match (a match without a predetermined outcome) with the Great Gotch, who eventually retired as an unbeaten champion. In 1920, Earl Caddock and Joe Stecher flip-flopped the title. Then, in December of 1920, Ed "Strangler" Lewis, a master of the sleeper hold, beat Stecher for the gold. Stanislaus Zbyszko, Gus Sonnenberg, Wayne Munn, and Stecher all held belts throughout the 1920s.

Amid much controversy, Dick Shikat defeated the "Golden Greek" Jim Londos in Philadelphia on August 23, 1929 to win the National Wrestling Association title. This first NWA was an offshoot promotion formed by a conglomerate of promoters. It was first known as the National Boxing Alliance and continued to promote throughout World War II. But with boxing becoming the nation's sport, the public kept wrestling on the back burner. Shikat, Londos, Sonnenberg, Lewis, and Ed Don George held versions of this title though the 1930s. Danno O'Mahoney, after defeating the likes of Londos, George, and Lewis all within one month in 1935, claimed the universal title at this time. However, in 1936, Shikat rose again to beat O'Mahoney.

Ali Baba beat Shikat in 1936, which became penny arcade view-master attraction. The machine had clips of the event and a customer plunked in a penny, turned the crank, and picture by picture, could view the event. In June 1936, in Cleveland, Everett Marshall beat Baba. On December 29, 1937, Lou Thesz captured the title for the first time. He lost to Crusher Casey in 1938 in Boston. In 1939, Thesz regained the title, but dropped it to Bronko Nagurski a few months later. From 1940 through 1947, NWA champions were plenty. Nagurski, Whipper Watson, and Thesz were among several warriors who captured gold.

promoters who were picking up steam in cities across America. Thesz was anointed champion in 1947 and defended the title with honor until 1966. His reigns for the new NWA highlighted the sport's appeal. Ric Flair, Terry Funk, Harley Race, Ricky Steamboat, Jack Brisco, and Shohei Giant Baba all held the prestigious belt.

Former WCW champ Booker T.

A bloody Hollywood Hogan with the WCW title.

WWF champ Mankind (Mick Foley).

The National Wrestling Alliance, the one that most fans know today, began in 1948. Again, it was a conglomerate of wrestling

In the early 1990s, wrestling was undergoing major changes. Now, two organizations—the World Championship Wrestling and World Wrestling Federation—crowned world champions. For years, the NWA was woven into the fabric of Ted Turner's WCW, based in

Atlanta, Georgia. In an effort to distance its own company from the network of small-time promoters who still believed in the NWA, officials at WCW severed its relationship with the century-old organization. WCW went on to continue world-title status and the NWA all but dissolved. Several years later, the NWA was retrieved by a group of regional promoters in North America and Japan. Amazingly, in this climate of wrestling mega-promotions, the NWA continues through the efforts of these smaller promoters. Chris Candido, Dan Severn, Naoya Ogawa, and Gary Steele have all held the NWA title in recent years.

Fujinami and Ric Flair at a match signing in Tokyo in 1991, prior to their title-vs.-title match.

Bruno turns New York into Garden party

Through the 1950s to 1970s, Bruno Sammartino and Madison Square Garden had a common bond. Sammartino was probably the most lucrative drawing attraction the arena ever had. Sammartino, who was the main event of the most dangerous villains of the day, put together sell-out after sell-out against foes like Superstar Billy Graham and Stan Stasiak. This special advertising that was sent to area press marveled at the wonder of Sammartino's popularity in New York. Unique ad copy like this can be bought for $50 because it ties together two legends: a building and a man which captivated a city.

★ GREATEST ATTRACTION ★
IN THE
HISTORY OF MADISON SQUARE GARDEN

FRED BLASSIE
JULY 11, 1964
SOLD OUT

★

KILLER KOWALSKI
AUGUST 23, 1963
SOLD OUT

★

THE GREAT MORTIER
JUNE 21, 1963
SOLD OUT

GORILLA MONSOON
JUNE 6, 1964
SOLD OUT

★

DR. JERRY GRAHAM
MARCH 16, 1964
SOLD OUT

★

BUDDY ROGERS
MAY 17, 1963
SOLD OUT

BRUNO SAMMARTINO

WORLD WIDE WRESTLING FEDERATION
HEAVYWEIGHT CHAMPION

WALDO VON ERICH
OCT. 19, 1964
SOLD OUT

★

GENE KINISKI
NOV. 16, 1964
SOLD OUT

★

TARZAN TYLER
SEPT. 27, 1965
SOLD OUT

BRUNO SAMMARTINO

HAS ALSO SUCCESSFULLY DEFENDED HIS TITLE AGAINST MANY OTHER OUTSTANDING INTERNATIONAL WRESTLING STARS AND HAS DRAWN GATE RECEIPTS OF MORE THAN $2,000,000 IN MADISON SQUARE GARDEN.

COWBOY BILL WATTS
OCT. 20, 1965
SOLD OUT

★

BIG BILL MILLER
AUGUST 2, 1965
SOLD OUT

★

GIANT BABA
FEB. 17, 1964
SOLD OUT

49

American Wrestling Association holds its own

But the NWA wasn't the only title. Politics of deciding who would carry the tile caused major rifts among some deserving wrestlers. So, in August 1960, Midwest promoters in particular became antsy. A 30-year-old University of Minnesota standout wrestler and football player, Verne Gagne, had been campaigning throughout the wrestling world. Major title shots and victories seemed to elude the Golden Gopher alumnus. Gagne rivaled Thesz as being the Upper Midwest's top-drawing attraction. As legend has it, Gagne aligned himself with a handful of promoters, bought the rights to the territory in Minneapolis-St. Paul, and made himself the world champion. With promoter Wally Karbo's brilliant sense of booking and his innate sense of getting along with people, wrestling in the Twin Cities spurned another new era for the sport.

From 1960 to 1990, the AWA was ruled by the Gagne family. Verne was the first champion and brother-in-law Larry Zbyszko was the promotion's last when the empire closed. Today, the greatest legacy left by the AWA is the memories. For 30 strong years, they were recognized in all corners of the world and by all major wrestling magazines. Verne had a good run to be certain.

For the better part of those 30 years, the AWA ruled the Midwest and parts of Canada and Japan. The superstars included the Crusher, Jim Brunzell, Rick Martel, Greg Gagne, the Hennigs, and the one and only, Baron Von Raschke. The territory prided itself on having a solid in-ring style, but added a unique sense of humor—fans from the

Verne Gagne, left, and Mad Dog Vachon were both champions in the 1960s and 1970s.

area can't shake memories of Mad Dog Vachon building a casket for Jerry Blackwell, for instance. The group allowed newcomers (Ric Flair, Iron Sheik, Ricky Steamboat) a chance to get their feet wet; tag teams (High Flyers Jim Brunzell and Greg Gagne, Jesse Ventura and Adrian Adonis, Nick Bockwinkel and Ray Stevens, Crusher and Vachon) to shine; the world's top stars (Johnny Valentine, Ernie Ladd, the Freebirds, the Road Warriors, Abdullah the Butcher, Jimmy Snuka, Pat Patterson, Bruiser Brody) to spread their wings, and always delivered the goods to fans.

Dusty Rhodes uses a chair on Harley Race during an early 1980s match.

The champions of the AWA were strong technicians who ventured as far as Japan and defended their honor in wrestling hotbeds like St. Louis, Amarillo, Memphis, Chicago, Indianapolis, Denver, San Francisco, and Winnipeg. Through the years, Minneapolis was always home for the AWA. When the WWF broke territorial truces in the 1980s, the promotion fell victim to poor business deals and wound up turning off its loyal fan base with an inferior product. For a time, though, the AWA was a highly respected organization whose champion was one fitting the title of world champ.

Sammartino, the Garden, and the McMahon family

Madison Square Garden is one of America's sports meccas. From its earliest days to the present, it has been a haven for professional wrestling. Joe Frazier and Sugar Ray Robinson headlined shows there, but Bruno Sammartino, an Italian immigrant turned pro wrestler, owned the Garden.

Throughout most of the 1960s, the strongman from Abruzzi, Italy, played to sellout cards at the Garden and major arenas throughout the East Coast. New York-area promoter Jess McMahon, Philadelphia's Willie Gilzenberg, and many others played under the auspices of the NWA and AWA, using those champions as their own. Soon, Eastern promoters grew tiresome of the constant politicking. In 1963, they founded the World Wide Wrestling Federation, a precursor to today's WWF. McMahon's son, Vince Jr., was ready to take over his dad's company. Vince Jr. got his feet wet in the business by running errands, making posters, and announcing for his pop. When he finally took over the reigns for Vince Sr., Vince Jr. shortened the WWWF name by dropping "Wide" from its moniker and yet another new era was born.

Buddy Rogers was an ex-NWA U.S. champion and a hot AWA contender. Feeling crunched by politics and an inability to secure another crack at Thesz, the original "Nature Boy" topped the king of acrobats Antonino Rocca in April 1963 to win the WWWF title. On May 17, 1963, Sammartino dethroned Rogers at the Garden in less than 60 seconds. To this day, Bruno claims the match was real and fought straight down the middle. Rumors circulated that Rogers was suffering from a bad heart, but Sammartino denies the story. By defeating a top foe like Rogers so convincingly, Sammartino shook the world of wrestling. Through the entire 1960s, he was undefeated and held back a "who's who" in the sport. His specialty was destroying the monsters: Gorilla Monsoon, the "Big Russian" Nikolai Volkoff, and Killer Khan gave their best effort, only to go home with a loss. Sammartino is remembered as the master of the bear hug and he may be the only man ever to slam 600-pound Haystacks Calhoun.

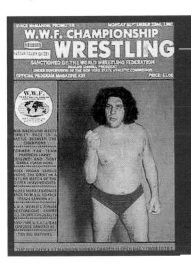

History of the sport found through programs

Wrestling programs are nearly gone, as both major promotions don't typically publish special-edition programs for pay-per-views or arena cards. As recently as the mid-1990s, the WWF was still selling collectible programs at all major supercards. During the 1980s, every promotion and territory sold them. During the 1970s and 1980s, virtually every major territory had the publishers at the Wrestling News develop the programs. These programs, like the one here with Andre the Giant on the cover, were sold in areas like the Mid-South to the AWA to the WWF. Today, collectors can expect to pay from $10 to $20 for a single program. However, special editions and ones that mark title changes are more valuable.

Bruno Sammartino puts a bear hug on Baron Scicluna.

The "Russian Bear" Ivan Koloff defeated Sammartino in January 1971. Pedro Morales beat Koloff two weeks later and held the belt for nearly three years until he fell victim to Stan Stasiak at the Spectrum in Philadelphia. Nine days later, Bruno outclassed Stasiak at the Garden to reclaim the world belt. He held the title for the next three years before losing to "Superstar" Billy Graham. Bruno's reign as the WWF champion was over. Many fans cried. At one time, the popular Italian rivaled Mickey Mantle as New York's top sports icon. He was so popular that, when national television did a series on sports legends, Bruno was included. He also was one of the few dual champions. Besides holding back all challenges for the WWWF world title, he held the tag-team titles for more than two years with Greek technician Spiros Arion. Sammartino and Arion defeated Lou Albano and Tony Altamore for the tag belts. Albano, later the greatest tag-team manager of any league, dedicated his life to dethroning Sammartino of the singles crown, but never succeeded.

Sammartino was a true gentleman in and out of the ring. He set the bar for champions. He was tirelessly active with numerous charities, often wore a suit and tie, and never shied away from the responsibilities of being a role model. Everyone who lived on the East Coast, wrestling fan or not, seems to have a favorite Bruno memory.

Indeed, fans of any league have vibrant memories of those champions. Thesz and Gagne were wrestling wizards and Sammartino was a brute. Today, wrestling fans are accustomed to seeing wrestlers like Kevin Nash and Dallas Page hold the WCW title, while Steve Austin and the Rock are kings of the WWF.

While they are certainly worthy performers themselves, the early days of the 1900s and up to the 1970s were an exciting, mysterious time in professional wrestling.

Former WWF champion Bret Hart.

A young X-Pac, right, then known as Lightning Kid, has a tug-of-war with Jerry Lynn over a title belt.

Tommy Rich, center, with Perry Saturn, left, and John Kronus, who were tag-team champs The Eliminators.

Shane Douglas is a former ECW world champion.

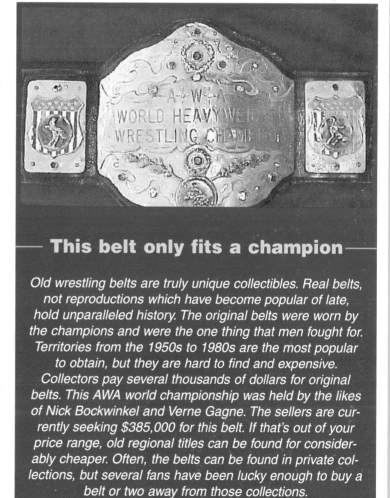

This belt only fits a champion

Old wrestling belts are truly unique collectibles. Real belts, not reproductions which have become popular of late, hold unparalleled history. The original belts were worn by the champions and were the one thing that men fought for. Territories from the 1950s to 1980s are the most popular to obtain, but they are hard to find and expensive. Collectors pay several thousands of dollars for original belts. This AWA world championship was held by the likes of Nick Bockwinkel and Verne Gagne. The sellers are currently seeking $385,000 for this belt. If that's out of your price range, old regional titles can be found for considerably cheaper. Often, the belts can be found in private collections, but several fans have been lucky enough to buy a belt or two away from those collections.

Al Snow shows off one of his most precious commodities.

Chapter 4

The Makings of a Wrestling Champion

Applying a neck lock, Whipper Watson shows why he was one of Lou Thesz's top foes.

Champions in wrestling, more so than any other field, have to be larger than life. The gold they wear cements that status. For the most part, wrestling champions are "wrestling" champions. World-class football players, weight lifters, karate stars, boxers, amateur wrestlers, and other sports stars have tried to chase wrestling-ring titles—most of them fail. For every amateur stand-out like Kurt Angle, there seems to be 20 Laurent Soucie's who couldn't make the transition from amateur to professional. For every celebrated football player, such as the Rock, Goldberg, and Ron Simmons, there are hundreds of ex-gridiron greats like Lawrence Taylor and Reggie White, who could barely lace up their boots. For every world-class weightlifter like Mark Henry or Ken Patera who do make the cut, there are thousands of men like Bill Kazmeier who simply don't make the grade.

Wrestling champions are rare breeds. Few in any field are as talented at what they do. They must adhere to long- and short-term promotional programs, be trustworthy and loyal employees, must be uniquely charismatic, and have athletic talent that few possess. Wrestling champions truly earn their moniker as the kings of sport. The wrestlers have to be special people to become true heroes or champions. Sex appeal is also important. A wrestler has to be appealing to women, but not too intimidating for men. The best champions are heroes who are better than most, but there also must be the illusion that he can be beaten by any wrestler on any night. It's easy to build a monster contender, but champions are very special. The fans must have in their minds that the match they are witnessing could be a title change—

Champions are the biggest focal point of any wrestling group. Throughout history, either the holder of the belt, the belt itself, or the chase to capture the belt has been the point of interest for the masses.

Today's wrestling builds larger-than-life stars, but there is no more compelling drama in sports than that of the chase for the championship. Some like Verne Gagne (AWA) start their own federation to get the gold. Others like Chris Benoit (WCW) chase the prize for years, only to walk away less than 24 hours later. Others, as in the case of the late Rick Rude, walk away from the ring after losing the belt in the final match of their career.

that's what makes the star worthy of having fans pay to see them. Baseball philosopher Branch Ricky once said, "You're only as good as your opponents and just a bit better than those you beat." In wrestling, that theory could not be more appropriate.

Good champions used to be people you could imagine your daughter bringing home with her. We trusted them and they left with us the feeling of good intentions. Using that line of thought, a case could be made for Bret Hart as being the greatest on-camera champion ever. Some insiders point to Thesz and Gagne. While some fans look to Hulk Hogan as the epitome of a star hanging on past his prime, perhaps it was Hogan's drawing power alone that made him the true King of the Ring.

In music, the greatest of the greats are known by their first or last name. Sinatra, Michael, Elvis, Garth, Madonna. In pro wrestling, the name also says it all—Thesz, Bruno, Cactus, Race, Inoki, Flair, Hogan, and Austin. Even the challengers are known with one name or a nickname—Abdullah, Lex, Kidman, Andre, and so on. We all have personal favorites. Like any other sport, declaring who is the greatest is subjective. Sports like baseball, boxing, and football have stats, but even they can be swayed to make a case. Wrestling has no such thing. Champions are indeed a special breed. In a sport where politics and behind-the-scenes-maneuvering and box office appeal play factors, being a champion is truly something special.

The case for Thesz and Flair

A strong case could be made for Thesz, the former NWA world champion. Ric Flair is said to have worn the NWA/WCW championship more than a dozen times throughout a 20-year span. Thesz, meanwhile, is merely a six-time title holder. Most fans who saw Thesz in his prime point to him as being the greatest champion the prestigious NWA ever

Lou Thesz maintains a hammerlock, as Larry Hennig applies a flying mare.

knew. Both Flair and Thesz were global champions. Thesz's longest title run was from 1948 to 1954. He also held the belt for three years, from 1963 to 1966. His other runs were short. Flair, on the other hand, never held the belt for more than two consecutive years. In the end, Thesz's overall years as champ dwarf Flair's reigns by comparison.

A billion arguments can be made for which star meant more for the sport. Flair wrestled a faster, harder pace—a by-product of the times. That style also left him open to more injuries, however. He also had to fend off threats by steroid-ridden powerhouses. Men like Flair thrive in today's wildly paced shows, whereas many champions of yesteryear couldn't have stayed popular in today's brand of wrestling. Athletically, Thesz could have, but he may have been forced to change his style through a steroid makeover.

In his prime, Thesz was considered to be a hunk. One popular sports magazine of the 1950s had a poll to decide who was the best-looking man in sports. Thesz rated third in an era where most of the media and press looked down at wrestling. Thesz had more than 5,000 matches with more than 500 men. Flair's totals are close to those. Both men were remarkably durable. Flair, to his credit, broke his back in a plane crash in the late 1970s and fought his way back to wres-

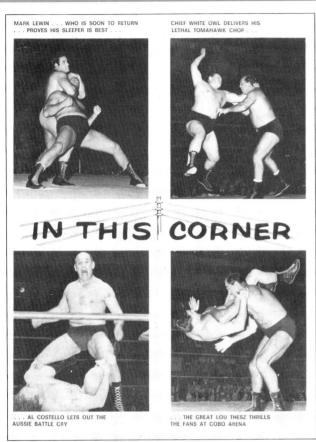

MARK LEWIN . . . WHO IS SOON TO RETURN . . . PROVES HIS SLEEPER IS BEST . . .

CHIEF WHITE OWL DELIVERS HIS LETHAL TOMAHAWK CHOP . . .

IN THIS CORNER

. . . AL COSTELLO LETS OUT THE AUSSIE BATTLE CRY

. . . THE GREAT LOU THESZ THRILLS THE FANS AT COBO ARENA

A 1960s program from Detroit's Cobo Hall.

tle when doctors questioned if he'd even walk again. Both wrestlers fought their way through the pro ranks without major pushes as preliminary performers.

Thesz is one of Japan's living legends. Flair's career was never based around the Orient, but he did do well on many tours there. Thesz is one of the only men to defeat four father-son combos. He held back challenges by Warren and Nick Bockwinkel, the Jonathans, Orville and Rich Brown, and the Funk family—Dory Sr., Dory Jr., and Terry. Thesz also beat numerous brother tandems like the Duseks and Sharpes. Thesz holds victories over world champions over a five-decade span. He remarkably had wins over Gorgeous George, Pat O'Connor, Killer Kowalski, Bill Watts, Gagne, Leo Nomellini, Whipper Watson, Dick the Bruiser, Bob Orton Sr., Buddy Rogers, Karl Gotch, Fritz Von Erich, and virtually every star of the NWA. He also held wins over England's Lord Layton and Japan's Giant Baba and Antonio Inoki on their home turf. One legend Thesz

did not defeat was Japan's father of professional wrestling, Rikidozan.

Flair makes his mark

Few men in any sport can claim the success that Flair can. Whether it's 12, 14, or 16 world titles—who is keeping count?—he's one of the most celebrated champions of all-time. It was through hard work and countless miles of traveling that made him a great.

After breaking into the business as a pudgy, 250-pound AWA rookie in the early 1970s, Flair seemed to be better suited for another career. After breaking his back in a near-fatal plane crash, Flair worked at rehabilitating. When he returned in the late 1970s, he earned main-event status and kept it through the Millennium.

Because the NWA belt was still recognized globally through the 1980s, Flair has been in more top-level feuds than any other wrestler alive. Take all of the top names of

Few men in any sport can claim the success that Ric Flair, one of the most celebrated champions of all-time, can.

the 1980s, throw them in a hat and Flair has probably wrestled them at one time or another. His wars with Ricky Steamboat, Harley Race, Bruiser Brody, the Funks, any member of the Von Erich family, Wahoo McDaniel, Sting, Dusty Rhodes, the Briscos, Ivan Koloff, Ron Garvin, and others kept NWA promoters alive in the 1980s.

In the 1990s, Flair ventured briefly to the WWF, where he expanded his list of opponents and cemented his name in the history books with feuds with Bret Hart, Randy Savage, Curt Hennig, and Roddy Piper. He returned to WCW in 1995, where he feuded further with top draws like Kevin Nash, Vader, Diamond Dallas Page, and Rick Rude. Crossing the generational gap has become an art for Flair, who has all but retired from active duty.

Ric Flair helps Sting work his abs.

Louis Thesz

A champion for the ages

Lou Thesz was a true-blue world champion. Thesz wrestled during an age when holding the NWA world title brought prestige and honor to the title bearer (1940s to 1960s). Amazingly, Thesz was crowned champion six times, a record before Harley Race topped that in the 1980s. A star in the U.S., Thesz also made a name for himself in Japan. Thesz collectibles are rare. His personal artifacts are in private collections and there are few commercially released items. This early 1960s Lou Thesz trading card is one of the few items of his that collectors can get their hands on. Thesz was also included in the early 1950s Parkhurst sets. Because it is so rare, collectors would expect to pay no less than $50 for this card.

Don't give collectibles like these the boot

When wrestlers retire, they hang up their boots. Naturally, when the boots are hung, a collector gets them somehow. These autographed Ric Flair boots, complete with the signature "RF" on the side, are owned by North Carolina fan West Potter. He paid several hundred dollars for these pieces of history. Boots have proven to be hot collectibles. Boots with special artwork (Hollywood Hogan's boots), designs (Iron Sheik's pointed-toe boots), or character (Steve Austin's plain black boots) are, and will be, worthwhile investments.

The Flair of a champion

There is a saying, "the clothes make the man," and former world champion Ric Flair certainly lived by that rule. Perhaps no wrestler at any time wore more outrageous, beautiful, and masterfully created ring robes than Flair. Flair had each of his several hundred robes hand-tailored by the late Olivia Walker. This robe, which is seen by many as his most memorable, was the sapphire-colored robe that Flair wore to the ring for his first NWA title win, a 1981 bout against Dusty Rhodes. In 1983, Flair wore the robe at his legendary Starrcade victory over Harley Race. Walker, who made robes and jackets for many wrestlers, needed three months to make this version of the "Nature Boy's" garment. Walker's artworks were special, indeed. She used peacock feathers and genuine Austrian rhinestones, all of which were affixed by hand. When completed, it weighed in excess of 40 pounds. Reportedly, Flair paid $4,500 to make this sapphire-colored version. Needless to say, the value of this historic piece is considerably higher than that. Collectors recently have paid several thousand dollars for other versions of Flair's robes.

Chapter 5

The '80s: MTV, the Von Erichs, and Saying Goodbye

The 1980s were a wacky and funky decade. MTV and the cable-television explosion made pop-culture icons out of one-hit-wonders.

In the early 1980s, wrestling territories were found in very region of the U.S. In that time, they were safe and sound. By the end of the decade, only the WWF and the Ted Turner-led WCW remained potent forces. After wrestlers could make a living in nearly 30 different promotions in every corner of the country, only Calgary Stampede, the AWA, Memphis, and Dallas groups led by Jerry Jarrett and Don Owens' Portland Championship remained. Old-time promoters were either bought by the WWF or forced to close shop. In the case of Fritz Von Erich's World Class Championship Wrestling and

Verne Gagne's AWA, they simply could not handle the competition from WWF and WCW. By this time, the two major groups were launching all-out assaults on regional territorial lines by touring nationally.

It was an interesting time to be a fan. If you lived in Chicago, you grew up watching promoter Fred Kohler's wrestling. For the first time, different groups were heading to Chicago and fans had their first chance to see new stars. It wasn't happening only in Chicago; it happened everywhere. The old-timer promoters in their hometowns felt the squeeze. In some cases, loss of talent caused promoters to unwittingly burn their fans before the promotion folded. The AWA, for example, refused to keep its available talent like the Road Warriors and after delivering top-caliber shows for nearly 25 years, out-of-shape losers and nonsensical storylines caused the AWA to pull the plug.

Although Greg Gagne was an exceptionally talented technician, fans of the 1980s found it hard to believe that a middle-aged, 180-pound, home-

Through the early 1980s, the famous Von Erich family had control of one of the hottest wrestling territories ever in Dallas. Three of the family members here are brothers Kevin, David, and Kerry.

town boy could beat 300-pound steroid monsters. Nor did fans believe that Verne, a 60-something tough guy, could beat wild men like Bruiser Brody. Verne made comeback and retirement tours so often that any credibility he had was eventually lost.

The Gagnes were not alone. Dozens of other long-time promoters insist that McMahon and Turner stole their talent and buried the small guys. The truth is, regional promoters had more than ample opportunity, talent, and resources to compete. In their last days, they simply made bad business decisions. It made it hard for fans to root for the home team. It was even harder, for the talent that stuck around through loyalty, to stay on a sinking ship any longer.

The Von Erich story

The Von Erich family in Dallas was a tragic story. Through the early 1980s, the family had control of one of the hottest territories ever. But one watching from the outside would not have envisioned the turmoil that lay inside. At one time, WCCW was seen on more than 80 networks worldwide. Fritz, an accomplished pro wrestler himself, owned the group, which used the Von Erich family sons as the main attractions. Mike, David, Kerry, and Kevin were the oyster in the eye of Dallas teen-agers. Sell-out crowds were a weekly guarantee and annual Super Cards at sold-out major arenas followed. The wrestling soon brought in fan worship to a

level that, at least locally, would rival any other hero than any sport. They were Elvis and the Dallas Cowboys rolled into one. More than 40,000 flocked to Texas Stadium to see David battle Ric Flair. With the kind of television exposure Von Erich had, WCCW had a chance to survive.

Family problems of the largest magnitude caused the territory's early demise, however. What happened to the Von Erich (Atkisson) family was something out of a nightmare. The beginning of the end came when the talented and powerful David died while touring Japan, and rumors of the family having abused drugs soon followed. Losing the top draw in any territory to death is not only tragic, but bad for business. Papa Fritz then crossed the line of good taste and charged more than 5,000 fans money to attend

The Fabulous Freebirds had career performances during the 1980s and cemented their place in history as the greatest working unit in wrestling history.

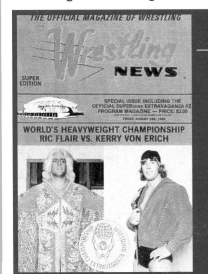

The night Kerry caught up with Ric

Ric Flair was right in the thick of his reign as NWA world champion when, in 1983, he met Kerry Von Erich in a series of matches that culminated at the Parade of Champions show in Texas in 1984. Beforehand, Von Erich had chased Flair all around the world in pursuit of the belt. This program, from their match at the Louisiana Superdome in 1984, chronicles that title chase. Programs like these can be found for $10 to $25. Von Erich finally got the better of Flair in Irving, Texas at a show to pay tribute to the late David Von Erich, his brother. Nearly 40,000 fans crushed into Texas Stadium to see Kerry win his only NWA title.

The Road Warriors, Animal, left, and Hawk were also a top tag team during the 1980s.

David's funeral. Later, Fritz profited greatly from the David Von Erich Memorial Show and fans started catching on.

Shortly thereafter, main-event star Gino Hernandez died from a drug overdose. The promotion hung tight, but drugs riddled the territory. Within several years, Mike, Kerry, and later the youngest, Chris, all committed suicide.

Through much of the 1980s, World Class was as hot as any promotion could be. The promotion could do no wrong. The Fabulous Freebirds had career performances there and cemented their place in history as the greatest working unit in wrestling history.

Veterans like Iceman Parsons, Bill Irwin, Ken Mantel, Skandor Akbar, Gary Hart, Jimmy Garvin, One Man Gang, Chris Adams, the Fantastics, and Eric Embry found new legs for themselves in World Class. Newcomers like the Simpsons, the Dingo Warrior (Jim Hellwig, who later became WWF champion Ultimate Warrior), Jack Victory, John Tatum, Precious, Sunshine, and later, Steve Austin, all received opportunities to hone their skills in the territory.

In the end, wrestling geniuses Jerry Jarrett and Jerry Lawler of Memphis tried to save the dying territory. They bought into the group, renamed it USWA, and hung tough

— SI gives wrestling credibility —

Only two wrestlers ever made the cover of Sports Illustrated: Danny Hodge did in 1957 and Hulk Hogan appeared in 1985 during the wrestling boom. When Hogan made the cover, it was a major story in the wrestling community. More than an exposé of the sport, the article dealt with the pageantry of wrestling and the pending Wrestlemania show. Mint copies of the issue can be found for $100. Will wrestling fans have to wait another 20 years before one of its stars makes the cover of SI again? Who knows. Until one is featured again, this issue will be a wrestling fan's most sought-after popular magazine for some time.

with an ESPN contract. Global Wrestling (1989-92) gave a valiant effort to jump start the area. They focused on ring work and gave Sean Waltman (X-Pac) and ECW mainstay Jerry Lynn a chance to show the world that little guys deserved a chance on the main stage. Eventually, no matter how hard Global tried, it had to accept the inevitable death of the territory.

In Canada, Bruce Hart nobly tried to keep his father's Stampede Promotions afloat. After a mid-1980s WWF buyout and returning to the family, Stampede lost most of its proven stars to the WWF. The team Badd Company (Brian Pillman and Bruce Hart), the unbeatable powerhouse Larry Cameron, technician Chris Benoit, and the ever-changing Blackhearts (Gangrel and Florida's Tom Nash) did their best to save the fledgling territory; but in 1991, poor box-office gates forced Stu Hart to pull the plug on the six-decade-old group. Down but not out, Bruce revived Calgary in late 1999 and utilized the likes of Sabu to breathe new air into the region.

Out West, one of the oldest surviving groups was Don Owens' Portland Championship Wrestling. Somewhere, the small town appeal of the group was lost with the fans. During the years it operated, a laundry list of wrestling greats traveled through the area. Roddy Piper cut his teeth in Portland before leaving for greener pastures in Georgia and later the WWF. Buddy Rose, Jesse Ventura, Dutch Savage, Col. DeBeers, and others all wrestled locally for the group which was an ally of the NWA. Often the NWA world champion like Thesz and Ric Flair made cameos there. In the later 1980s, Tom Zenk, Curt Hennig, Nord the Barbarian, Scott Norton, and the late Art Barr as Beetlejuice tried their best to salvage what was left of the dying group. Eventually, small gates, lack of sponsorship, and having no solid TV contract forced Owens to say goodnight.

The 1980s saw industry changes—many good and many bad. Many fans will forever miss the territories. Although Memphis and Ohio Valley Championship Wrestling (Jim Cornette's group) are alive mainly through working relationships with the WWF as a feeder group, the 1980s marked the last decade in an 80-year span where the territorial system ruled in North America.

This family owned Dallas and the early 1980s

The Von Erich wrestling clan was at its peak in the 1980s out of Dallas' World Class Wrestling. In real life they were the Adkisson family. Truly, the sons of Fritz Von Erich, a star from the 50s and 60s, were tremendous athletes. Kerry was a state high school champion in track and field. All five sons got into the wrestling business and followed in dad's footsteps. The boys were mega-stars in the early 80s, regularly selling out arena in Dallas-Ft. Worth. They were a hit with young females all around the Southwest. Not many items from their days are available, but this Von Erich board game is one unique item. The game is rare. This one was found for $100 in good shape. Sadly, the family's history had a tragic ending due to substance abuse (See above chapter). But their memorable legacy will live on forever.

Chapter 6

Tough Guys and Heroes

What exactly is a hero? Whatever makes one, there is no denying that true heroes will always be bigger-than-life figures. World Wrestling Federation promoter Vince McMahon Jr. calls his heroes "live-actions stars." He could not be more correct.

While McMahon's outlook on wrestling fits today's scene, from the turn of the century through the 1990s, heroes were simply honest men and women who battled for good over evil. The heroes of wrestling's earliest days were part John Wayne, part Lionel Barrymore, and part Gary Cooper. They were good looking fellows who, while kindhearted away from the ring, could deftly battle any size monster that promoters threw at them.

To be a well-rounded pro wrestler in any era, one needs to be legitimately tough, both physically and mentally. Wrestlers must also be extremely talented and have a knack for storytelling. The best heroes

Hulk Hogan strikes a heroic pose.

told a story in their matches, much like a Hollywood movie. The parallels between Hollywood and wrestling are striking. Wrestling has made a habit of taking a dose of Hollywood fantasy and translating it into the ring.

As movie heroes became more flawed—take Marlon Brando, James Dean, and later, Charles Bronson and Clint Eastwood, for example—so went the heroes of wrestling. From the beginning days of world champions through the 1960s, heroes generally played their part to a tee. They were Wayne, Barrymore, and Cooper all the way. Throw in an amateur wrestling background and an all-star was born.

Part of the allure of heroes and tough guys was their believability. If fans believed the hero was tough enough to battle any wild man a promoter threw at him, that wrestler could go far and gain mass appeal.

Wrestling's days of Frank Gotch and Joe Stecher were a time of honest contested fights. When exactly wrestling changed from this type of performance (called a shoot) to pre-determined outcomes (a work) is difficult to pinpoint. Real ring wars were held in the U.S. at least through the 1920s. In Japan, the UWF's late 1980s fights were also sold as real, as are today's versions—Pancrase, UFO, and K-1. Ironically, the century began with the majority of wrestling matches being contested for real. At the end of the century, wrestling had come full circle. Fans were becoming better educated by insider publications and the Internet. Even wrestlers and promoters, who no longer had connections to the old days, openly talked about the legit-

Goldberg checks his press coverage in the Japanese magazines.

outs or barroom brawlers like Dr. Death (Steve Williams), Hacksaw Duggan, John Nord, and Rick Steiner. Watts recently said in a video-taped interview that he liked having tough men as part of the UWF. He quipped about the crew after-hours, "I didn't care at all if they got into a bar fight, but if they lost, I would fine them on the spot."

Oklahoma great Danny Hodge is considered a legendary tough guy. The former pro was a national champion at Oklahoma State and is the only wrestler to hold both national AAU wrestling and boxing championships simultaneously. Prior to a shoulder injury, when he turned to pro wrestling full-time, Hodge had compiled a 12-1 record as a pro boxer. Before his injury, he was mere months away from a title shot and may very well have won a championship in boxing. Remembered as the finest light heavyweight champion ever, Hodge wrestled in a career filled with historic one-hour-long matches. Oftentimes, he gave up in excess of 30 pounds to his opponents while wrestling in the heavyweight division. It was a rarity when Hodge was pinned cleanly. Hodge is remembered also for what he didn't do—but was capable of doing—in the ring. He could legitimately hurt his foes if he chose, but mostly he spared them of significant injury. That perceived violence which he inflicted on his opponent typifies the attraction fans have to wrestling.

imacy of wrestling. Promoters and scriptwriters actually used the "is it real or not" idea to their advantage by writing it into weekly storylines. The New World Order, Steve Austin vs. Vince McMahon, and may other angles were a result of this new twist.

Toughness is always a big sell. Bill Goldberg's power and Austin's defiance are versions of new age toughness. Former promoter Bill Watts was legendary for having tough guys in his Mid-South and UWF territories. Watts loved to utilize amateur stand

The Body gets stuck on fans 3

Jesse "The Body" Ventura had brand-name appeal even before he won the Minnesota governor's seat in Minnesota in 1999. For that reason, Ventura merchandise is valuable commodity for collectors. Jesse, as he is known by his closest associates, has been a mastermind at branding his character. He wrote a best-selling book, has appeared in several big budget films, and even has his own line of action figures. When Jesse first left the AWA for the WWF in 1984, little did he know the chance he was taking to join the league would turn out so well. Early Ventura collectibles are not plentiful and items that are available are tough to find. This sticker is included in the Topps 1987 WWF Sticker set that sells for $10.

JESSE VENTURA

From the gridiron to the ring

Athletes come no tougher than wrestlers and football players. Combine an athlete who is adept at both and someone special emerges. Football players have always had a deep connection to professional wrestling. Promoters have used ex-gridiron stars to boost attendance, either for one-time main events or as regular performers.

Chicago Bears Hall of Fame fullback Bronko Nagurski is perhaps the most celebrated pro wrestler of all-time. In between his football seasons during the '30s and '40s, Nagurski would wrestle. Often called the greatest football player to ever live, Nagurski also won three wrestling world championships before he retired. When sportswriters asked him about his days in the ring, the University of Minnesota football star didn't say much other than it marked a "degrading" time in his life. History books note Nagurski mostly for his playing days. But in wrestling, he was more than just an oddball attraction. He was one of the great wrestlers, too.

In subsequent years, many ex-football players made lives for themselves in the ring. Many only got as far as college, but a few came from the pro ranks to join wrestling.

Gus Sonnenberg was a tackle at Dartmouth college. When he turned pro, Sonnenberg utilized football techniques in the ring such as the flying tackle. Although promoters clearly pushed his All-American status, he was known to fans as the "Human Torpedo." Others were fortunate to play in the NFL. Leo Nomellini was also an All-American at Minnesota who played 14 seasons with the San Francisco 49ers. Like Nagurski, Nomellini is in the Hall of Fame. Ed "Wahoo" McDaniel, one of the all-time great Native American stars, played defense for the New York Jets and Miami Dolphins and wrestled during the off-season. After football, he was trained further by Dory Funk

Bronko Nagurski is another football star turned wrestling champion.

Sr. and went on to a 20-year career as a wrestler.

Even today, many stars have football backgrounds. Bill Goldberg (Atlanta Falcons), Darren Drozdov (Denver Broncos), Lawrence Taylor (New York Giants), Kevin Green (Pittsburgh Steelers), and Reggie White (Green Bay packers) have all tried wrestling, to varying degrees of success. Goldberg became an icon in wrestling and Drozdov was settling into his career when an injury in the ring sadly paralyzed him from the chest down. Taylor, Green, and White were special attractions in the WWF and WCW and Green even warned he may join wrestling full-time. Currently, the WWF has four former college football stand outs (Farooq, Bradshaw, Austin, and The Rock).

Originators of the sport

Native Americans are truly heroic figures in wrestling. Not only for their talents, but for their battles against stereotyping that has long permeated the industry.

"Indians were always talented wrestlers," said Bruce Hart, Calgary Stampede promoter and brother of Bret Hart. "They're also great drawing cards. There was a time when virtually every promoter had to have an Indian in the show."

But those opportunities were also met with classi stereotyping. Billy Red Cloud, Sonny War Eagle, Don Eagle, Wahoo McDaniel, and Tiny Mills were Native Americans who did not have a choice. Until recently, they were barely accepted by society in any acceptable manner. If promoters told McDaniel to be called "Wahoo," McDaniel had few options. Once Native Americans got

Gus Sonnenberg helped solidify wrestling's image.

in the ring, it was magic. They lit up crowds from coast to coast. McDaniel was perhaps the greatest of all. Over the course of his career, McDaniel was a star in Florida, the AWA, and the NWA, where he feuded with Ric Flair. Years later, McDaniel realized he would be best suited in tag-team competi-

Ali and Inoki in a bout for the ages

Muhammed Ali had to give it a try. In 1976, the former boxing champion shocked the world by taking on professional wrestlers.

This marked the first time in history that a current heavyweight champion would try wrestling while still in the prime of his career. With warm-up bouts against Gorilla Monsoon and Kenny Jay under his belt, Ali was ready to take on the pride of Japan, Antonio Inoki. Ali was reportedly paid several million dollars to appear and Inoki knew that a match against Ali would make him an instant legend. What really happened in the match is uncertain. Some call it a real match, others do not. In the U.S., fans paid up to $50 apiece to witness the match on closed-circuit television. For 15 rounds, Inoki laid on his back and mostly kicked at Ali's thighs, which took away the boxer's skills. Thirty years later, the match has become a famed chapter in Inoki's career. For collectors, the bout is a favorite. Posters of the show can be found for under $200, and video of the match can be found for under $50. Today, Inoki is retired, but his name lives on. This doll continues to sell for about $45.

tion. He brought Jules Strongbow to the NWA with him and had success. Prior to that, Vince McMahon Sr. used Billy White Wolf as Strongbow's partner in the WWF. Together, they were a very popular team.

Over half of the so-called Native Americans who entered the ring were not even 1/16 true Indians. But if promoters could convince fans an ex-Olympian named Maurice Vachon was a "Mad Dog," telling fans that a darker-skinned wrestler with a headdress was an Indian wasn't a far-fetched idea. Many American Indians were actually Mexicans. Even though Mexican wrestlers could be headliners in their home-land, few made the kind of money American wrestlers were taking in in the U.S. When second-generation wrestlers Mark and Chris Romero were at a career crossroads, they allowed promoters to turn them into "Youngbloods." Jay Youngblood was a popu-lar NWA star who died at a young age. When Mark and Chris came along, fans knew the name and instantly took to the brothers. They didn't reach the success that Jay Youngblood attained, but the brothers did have numerous tours in World Class, Japan, Puerto Rico, and South Africa.

Billy White Wolf.

Billy Whitewolf, right, and Chief Jay Strongbow were a formidable force.

Ironically, a Native American with an Hispanic name, Chris Chavis, was the top-drawing Indian in the 1990s. As Tatanka—a name given to him after the movie "Dances With Wolves"—he was the WWF interconti-nental champion. After touring with the WWF, he stayed active on the independent circuit. Steve Gatorwolf was a WWF prelimi-nary performer in the mid-1980s and now runs a training facility in his native Arizona. The late Little Beaver was one of the most popular midget wrestlers of all-time. He was a widely used talent in the 1960s and didn't retire until the 1980s. Whether it's McDaniel or Tatanka, Native Americans have always lent something magical to wrestling. Hollywood is beginning to throw away old stereotypes and hopefully pro wrestling will bring some respect to Native Americans in the future.

An original, a governor, and a giant

In Japan, Rikidozan, Antonio Inoki, and Giant Baba were the three biggest heroes ever. Rikidozan was a former Sumo wrestling star who rose to power in the 1950s. In 1953, Lou Thesz traveled to Japan to capture the first Japan Wrestling Association NWA International belt. Five years later, Rikidozan became the champion and wrestling in that country escalated to new heights. He later became a promoter in Japan and brought in top challengers from around the world to wrestle. His matches with the Destroyer and Fred Blassie were classic bloodbaths. Blassie was relentless in his pursuit of Rikidozan's belt and tried to bite his way to victory. By the 1960s, Rikidozan slowed and turned his attention to grooming his successors, Shohei "Giant" Baba and Antonio Inoki.

Baba, at 6 foot 9, 260 pounds, was a gangly-looking wrestler who turned to the ring when he failed at making it in Japan's professional baseball league. When Rikidozan was murdered in late 1963, both Baba and Inoki were left to fill his monumental shoes. Baba first won the JWA/NWA title in 1965.

Bruno Sammartino and Pedro Morales were both top stars from the 1960s and 1970s and popular with fans, and the two wrestlers once faced each other in the ring, which ended with a 75-minute draw.

He lost the belt to Bobo Brazil in 1968, only to win it back two days later in Tokyo. In the fall of 1972, Baba left the promotion to form

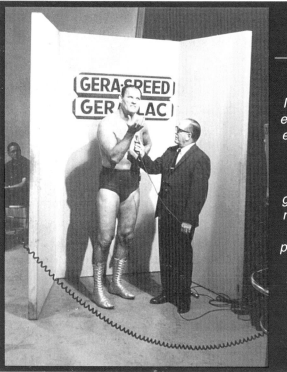

Pitchmen who knew a thing about selling

It wasn't uncommon for wrestlers, even in the sport's earliest days, to be pitchmen. Frank Gotch did it with his patented "Gotch Socks." By the time the 1950s rolled around and television wrestling was a hit, wrestlers increasingly attached their names to different products. One product was Gera-Speed, an apothecary product that was said to give a person more vitality. Verne Gagne was once a pitchman for the product, seen here on a billboard behind Killer Kowalski and announcer Marty O'Neill. Today, wrestlers pitch everything from ravioli to credit cards. Advertising artifacts from the 1950s that include wrestlers can be found though Internet auctions for a wide range of prices. Small articles can be bought for $25.

his own group, All-Japan, where he won no fewer than six singles titles. He was the NWA world champion three times and competed regularly through the 1990s.

Inoki also opened his own promotion, New-Japan wrestling, with friend and actor Seiji Sakaguchi. Inoki won a wide array of belts and wrestled numerous boxers and martial artists. He defeated Andre the Giant for his first Grand Prix belt in a 1983 tournament. Throughout Inoki's career, he battled most of the top Japanese and American stars and even beat former boxing champion Leon Spinks. In the late 1980s, Inoki battled Mr. Saito in an "island match" that lasted nearly an entire day. Saito, who had just returned to Japan, played the ultra-villain. After Saito and Ken Patera were jailed for two years in Wisconsin for assault, Saito was scheduled to return to Japan to dethrone and embarrass Inoki. The only people who attended this pre-"Survivor" battle were press members and fellow wrestlers. A ring was set up on an island and both competitors were brought to the island by boat. The wrestlers camped out in tents for nearly a

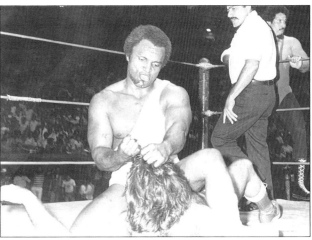

Carlos Colon about to slug Dutch Mantell, circa mid-1980s..

day until they were both ready for the match. More than the match itself, the event was promoted in a four-hour television special. The show, in which Inoki prevailed, was a hit and is now popular with collectors. Inoki also beat Jesse Ventura to politics. In the 1990s, Inoki was selected to be part of the Japanese Diet, an equivalent of the U.S. Senate.

While Baba was no politician, he was Inoki's equal in terms of being an icon. When Baba passed away in 1999, his funeral was carried on live television and attended by 50,000 Japanese fans.

Morales, Colon, and the best of Puerto Rico

There have been numerous wrestlers of Puerto Rican heritage. But the biggest stars to come from the island are Pedro Morales and Carlos Colon. Morales captured the hearts of American fans in 1971 by winning the WWF championship from Russian Ivan Koloff at Madison Square Garden. Morales fended-off any challenge thrown at him by different managers—everything from bullies to monsters to weirdos. Eventually, the manager the Grand Wizard dethroned Morales with the help of Stan Stasiak in 1973.

Seven years later, Morales beat Ken Patera to become the intercontinental champion. That was a title that Morales would trade back and forth with Don Muraco in the

Giant Baba and The Sheik in a fearsome battle from the 1970s.

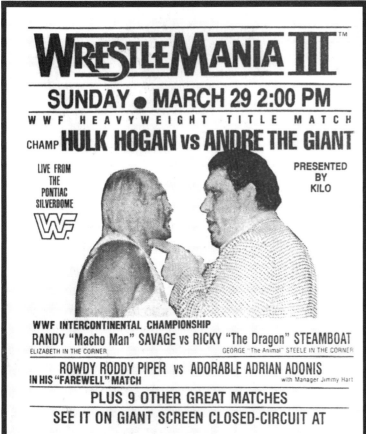

WRESTLEMANIA III™

SUNDAY • MARCH 29 2:00 PM

WWF HEAVYWEIGHT TITLE MATCH

CHAMP **HULK HOGAN** vs **ANDRE THE GIANT**

LIVE FROM THE PONTIAC SILVERDOME

PRESENTED BY KILO

WWF INTERCONTINENTAL CHAMPIONSHIP

RANDY "Macho Man" SAVAGE vs RICKY "The Dragon" STEAMBOAT
ELIZABETH IN THE CORNER   GEORGE "The Animal" STEELE IN THE CORNER

ROWDY RODDY PIPER vs ADORABLE ADRIAN ADONIS
IN HIS "FAREWELL" MATCH   with Manager Jimmy Hart

PLUS 9 OTHER GREAT MATCHES

SEE IT ON GIANT SCREEN CLOSED-CIRCUIT AT

The Silverdome is full and rocking

Vince McMahon saw dollar signs when he dreamed of pitting Hulk Hogan against Andre the Giant in 1987—and what better showcase than Wrestlemania III? What better venue than the 90,000-seat Pontiac Silverdome? More than 70,000 fans packed the dome to take part in history. It was a mega-event on pay-per-view, as it attracted the biggest worldwide audience ever for a wrestling show. Hogan retained his title by pinning Andre in the main event. But it was more than a one-match show. Ricky Steamboat and Randy Savage pit on a classic Intercontinental title match, and who can forget King Kong Bundy giving three midget wrestlers a body splash? Because it is still the most recognized wrestling show of all-time, merchandise from the event sells for a premium, but T-shirts, programs, and posters can be found for $30.

early 1980s. At one time, Morales was the first man to hold the WWF's world title, intercontinental title, and tag-team title. In an era when Sammartino left large shoes to fill, the WWF sorely needed to keep crowds interested. Morales did what was needed and then some.

Colon traveled throughout the U.S. in the 1970s, but was he learning his trade or actually scouting talent? Stateside success had eluded Colon, but when he returned to Puerto Rico, he passed all wrestlers as the top drawing card. Colon reportedly bought a stake in the World Wrestling Council. But like many other promoting wrestlers, he earned the respect of fans and peers. In WWC, Colon won the championship on many occasions. He regularly fought American challengers which he had run across in his times wrestling in the U.S. He wrestled Harley Race, Ric Flair, Junkyard Dog, Jerry Lawler, Eddie Gilbert, and Dutch Mantel. Although Colon did well against technicians like Rick Martel, he was best suited battling the

strong heels. Colon made brawling outside the ring with his opponents a trademark of Puerto Rican wrestling. Action in Puerto Rico was ultra-extreme. His rivalries with heels Dick Murdoch, Dusty Rhodes, Bruiser Brody, Gorilla Monsoon, Kimala, Randy Savage, Hercules Ayala, and Abdullah the Butcher were all mat classics. Nowadays, his son Carly has taken over the Colon legacy.

Back to where it started

Today's wrestling heroes haven't changed all that much. Though our good champions may have a harder edge, they are basically the same wrestlers who performed as Steve Williams, Giant Baba, and Pedro Morales.

Steve Austin and the Rock are heroes for the new age. The are multi-layered personalities. Through interviews and matches, they convey a certain aura that is pure hero. Austin is a hero for his confidence and defiance of authority. The Rock is a hero for his unwavering bravery. Goldberg is a hero for his power and simplicity in the ring.

Olympic star Chris "Supersplash" Taylor, who weighed in at 485 pounds, was popular in the 1970s.

Today, fans are much closer to their stars than they were in years previous. Fans know every detail about the lives of these wrestlers, which adds to their appeal. Most of all, none of today's heroes will turn down an opportunity to fight the biggest challenger of the moment. When Triple H challenged Austin and Rikishi challenged the Rock, or when Scott Steiner challenged Booker T, those heroes not only accepted the matches for themselves: In a way, they accepted on behalf of the fans. That feeling fans get that a hero, tough guy, or champion is taking on an opponent for their sake, is a reason why wrestling is so widely watched today.

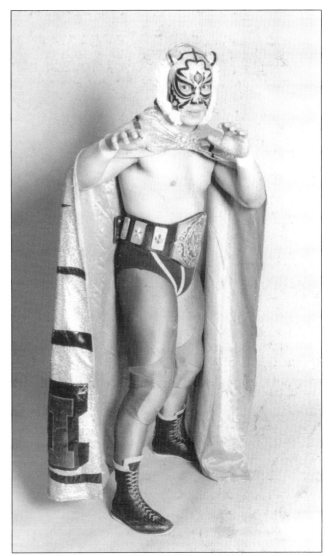

Tiger Mask was a popular wrestler with fans.

Gene Kiniski assumes the traditional defense position, as Pat O'Connor gains the upper hand.

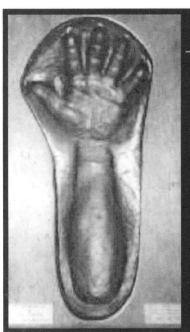

An exclusive item from a real legend

Andre Rene Roussimoff was wrestling's true larger-than-life figure. Still known as the most popular wrestling attraction the world has ever had, Andre the Giant once made a caste of his uniquely large hand and forearm. Andre's hands were so large, he is often remembered for drinking his beer straight from a pitcher because he could not hold a glass. This special artifact was caste as a gift to former Houston promoter Paul Boesch. When Boesch passed away, the caste wound up in the private collection of former AWA world champion Nick Bockwinkel. Today, the artifact is up for auction on the Internet. The current owners list the Andre caste at a cool $1.2 million, easily making it the most valuable wrestling artifact.

Mick Foley as Mankind, left, and when he was Cactus Jack, at right.

The many moods and makeup of Sting.

Verne Gagne was one of the all-time wrestling heros.

Harley Race was a classy NWA champion.

Jesse Ventura flexes some muscle.

Terry Funk is a four-decade grappler and a true legend.

Bob Backlund and Peter Maiva, The Rock's grandfather. Backlund was a WWF champ in the early 1980s.

Dingo Warrior with Gary Hart.

Jerry "The King" Lawler put Memphis wrestling on the map.

Magnum T.A. was a NWA super-star in the early 1980s

Sid Vicious has size and power behind him.

Famed NWA champion Pat O'Connor always played the good guy.

Tully Blanchard is a sec-ond-generation star.

Mil Mascaras flexing his muscles.

Tough Guys and Heroes

Andre the Giant hoists a bevy of beauties. Few wrestlers had more world-wide appeal than Andre.

Hulk Hogan with arch nemesis Jesse Ventura.

Title winner Ricky Steamboat was a superb technician.

Former Mid-South champ Ted DiBiase was usually a favorite with the fans.

Top NWA star Jack Brisco was respected in and out of the ring.

Title winner and strongman Ken Patera.

Chapter 7

Parts Unknown: Wrestlers From Faraway Places

Prior to the 1980s, wrestling fans were left in the dark as to the what, where, and why about their favorite wrestlers, particularly villains. What were they really about? Where did they live? Did they have families? Why did they choose wrestling? Those were honest questions to ask. After all, fans only saw one side of the wrestler, the one on television. Was the wrestler named Kabuki really a Ninja warrior from Japan? Was the Iron Sheik really a national hero in his native Iran? Were these stories that fans heard on television real? Until the late 1980s, promoters believed that if the fans really knew that, say, Gorilla Monsoon wasn't found in some Asian village devouring witless foes, as was said about him on television, nobody would pay to see him wrestle.

That continues today. In WWF storylines, the Undertaker accidentally burned his family as a child. His younger "brother," Kane, now wears a mask to cover those burns. In real life, Kane (Glenn Jacobs) and Undertaker (Mark Calloway) are not brothers and no such story ever happened. The reason why promoters use these stories is simple: it sells tickets.

Most of the wrestlers who used "foreigner" gimmicks were actually from the United States. Baron Von Raschke was a goose-stepping heel with a German gimmick. Actually, he was from Nebraska. Sabu claims he is from the Far East and a descendent of a family of nasty sheiks. Actually, he is from Michigan. And on it goes.

Russians and Germans

Americans, it seems, love to hate. Racial stereotyping has been a way of life in Hollywood for years. Should it be expected that it would be any different in the wrestling ring? Performers from Germany and Russia fit right in. With the knowledge of Adolph Hitler's brutal reign in the 1940s, it was easy to jeer a wrestler using a Nazi gimmick. When World War II was finally over, the emotion of those years spilled over into wrestling

El Canek, a popular Mexican star, was one of the few wrestlers to ever pin Andre the Giant.

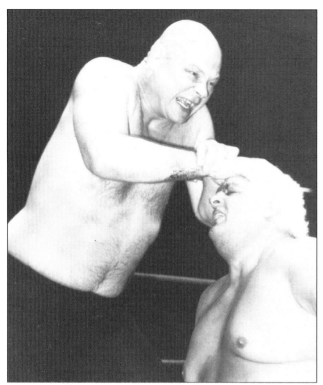

Baron Von Raschke puts his famous claw on Dusty Rhodes during a match from the 1970s.

Iraqi soldiers lined up in the ring after the match and shot so many bullets over our heads, it looked like the Fourth of July. When it was over, George told me that if he had hurt me, those soldiers would have shot him. I just smiled and never answered."

For much of his career, Gordienko's character was a rugged Russian who acted the part. The Volkoffs, Kamilkoffs, Krusher Kruschev (who was from Minneapolis), Ivan Koloff and his nephew Nikita (also from Minnesota), Boris Zukoff, and others were easy to get riled over.

Jim Raschke was a wrestling and football star in college from Omaha, Nebraska—former AWA promoter Verne Gagne loved to hire former all-American athletes with a background similar to his. As himself, Jim Raschke was dull and, being a logical thinker, he knew his career was going nowhere fast. After touring with colorful men like Dick the Bruiser, Bobby Heenan, Blackjack Lanza, and the Crusher, the 20-something Nebraska native changed his life forever. He shaved his head, borrowed the "claw" maneuver from fellow German character Fritz Von Erich, began talking in a German-like accent, and changed his name to Baron Von Raschke. In the 1970s, Baron stomped around rings worldwide. As a monster heel, he challenged many a champion like Gagne, Bruno Sammartino, and Antonio Inoki. He had longtime success in the AWA with Horst Hoffman as his partner. Toward

arenas. Germans and eventually Russians became the ring's biggest villains. While the Cold War continued, Russian gimmicks allowed fans an opportunity to both hate the heels and be patriotic toward the U.S. at their local arenas.

One such star who played the part of a Russian was George Gordienko. "Gordienko was the toughest S.O.B. I've ever met," said Sheik Adnan Al-Kaissey. "Wherever he went, the locals found a way to dodge fighting him. When I fought him in Iraq, it was insane. The

Movie stars of a different sort

In the late 1950s, Mexican wrestling star El Santo (the Saint) started a prosperous movie career. He went on to star in dozens of Mexican feature films through the 1980s that saw him use his wrestling persona against supernatural villains. The poster from this film (released in 1971), which translated into English means, "The Mummies of Guanajuato," also features wrestlers the Blue Demon and Mil Mascaras. Often these two wrestlers would co-star with El Santo. El Santo's movie paraphernalia is high in demand from cult-movie fans and this poster is selling for $50 in the United States. Unless you speak Spanish, watching El Santo's movies is something of a chore, as they are not translated into English. Even so, the El Santo movies make for fun collectors' items.

Dory Funk Jr. and Genichiro Tenyru.

plying the U.S. with talented opponents. Mitsu Arakawa, Kabuki, Kendo Nagasaki, Harold Sakata, Mr. Fuji, Ryuma Go, Toru Tanaka, The Great Muta, and a host of others have been an integral part of wrestling lore. Sadly, like virtually all ethnic backgrounds, the Japanese stars have been stereotyped mainly as heels. Rather than allow them to shine, American promoter were simply happy to let them be jeered. Japanese promoters, though, got the last laugh. Many Americans got their biggest paydays wrestling in the East. Putting the shoe on the other foot, Americans had to work twice as hard to be accepted there and work three times harder to win over the crowds. Many Americans were stereotyped as well and eventually had to lose to Japan's hometown heroes. Few Americans, however, were stereotyped as blatantly as Japanese stars in the U.S. Even today, talents like

the end of his career, when he aligned himself with fan favorites, the Baron became revered by fans. Today, he remains a cult hero on the independent circuit.

In Germany, no wrestling fan has been sheltered from the presence of real-life German native, Otto Wanz. Wanz, a hefty wrestler, is the owner of Germany's CWA promotion. Prior to promoting, Wanz shocked the world by winning the AWA belt in the early 1980s. It was the AWA where he was known to rip phone books in half. His feud with Nick Bockwinkel and Bobby Heenan turned the usually docile AWA rings into blood-soaked canvases. It was in the feud with Wanz that Heenan popularized his trademark fall as he ran away from his foe. Making Wanz look like a superhero overnight was no small task but Heenan pulled it off.

Land of the Rising Sun

Although Asian wrestlers have been some of the most talented found anywhere, they were always relegated to heel roles in the ring because of their ethnicity. Through the years, Japan has been a fertile land in sup-

Jumbo Tsuruta was one of Japan's most revered athletes during the 1980s.

Japanese hardcore legend Atsushi Onita.

Japanese star Masato Tanaka.

Tajiri brought several innovative moves with him when he came over from Japan to join ECW.

Fans flip over Mexican stars

In Mexico, Lucha Libre is as popular as wrestling in the United States and its history is just as long. Naturally, wrestling collectibles are sold in Mexico and fans can get anything from dolls to novelties to masks. This Lucha Libre puzzle is a new item and can be found on the Internet for $20. Interestingly, masks of the superstars are extremely popular. Well-made renditions of the masks worn by legends like El Santo, the Blue Demon, and Mils Mascaras and newcomers like Rey Mysterio Jr. and Psycosis can be found through vendors before the wrestling matches in Tijuana and Mexico City. Through mail order, U.S. fans can buy them as well. They range in price (depending on production difficulty) from $60 to $150.

Few were safe around tag-team champs Afa and Sika, better known as the Samoans.

Don "The Magnificent" Muraco was a favorite with fans during the 1970s.

Kaientai, Kaz Hayashi, and Magnum Tokyo are relegated to roles on the back burner.

The Wild Samoans

The Samoans, Afa and Sika, are seemingly related to every islander who has stepped into the ring. Wrestlers they weren't. Instead, they were all wild-eyed, bona-fide butt kickers. Afa and Sika were hardcore before hardcore was cool. Sometimes they were seen eating raw fish or talking in some strange dialect no one understood. In their wake, others followed. Rikishi, Tonga Kid, Samu, and the late Yokozuna all made an impact in wrestling. Rikishi is one of the new era's superior performers. His 15-foot leap off a cage onto Val Venis and his subsequent fall from off the Hell in a Cell into a pickup truck have proven to be classic moments in the year 2000.

The Rock, too, is related to the Samoan family tree. His well-documented tale of growing up with wrestling 24 hours a day was told in the New York Times bestseller, The Rock Says. His dad, Rocky Johnson, is a former WWF tag-team champion and his mom is the daughter of "High Chief" Peter Maivia, one of the WWF's top draws in the 1970s.

Though not related to the Samoan family tree, "Superfly" Jimmy Snuka may have been the top island star. He was a legitimate brawler who had a reputation amongst the other wrestlers for being one of the toughest men to ever step foot in a ring. He left many fans with an indelible memory after he leapt off a cage for the first time. Mick Foley even credits that death-defying leap for planting a seed in him to become a wrestler.

Don Muraco left the island of Hawaii with the good looks of Tom Selleck and the sculpted body of Rick Rude. In the early '70s, he worked most available circuits with only mid-level success. Once he gained weight, turned on the fans and declared himself to be "Magnificent." Muraco became a main-event caliber star wherever he went. As he shuffled down the aisle in a cocky manner, he would grab a microphone to insult the fans. Muraco became a one-of-a-kind character and won't be forgotten. Throughout the 1970s and 1980s, few threw insults or worked the crowd like he did. Prior to his final years in the industry, the Magnificent Muraco was a heel for the ages. Part 1950s, part 1980s, and 100-percent box office.

Don't forget the Sheiks

Arab stars were some of the most unique and mystical characters in wrestling. But there was more to their personalities than a turban and pointed boots. Sheiks have popped up in virtually every territory at some time. Some were legit Arabs and others just saw it as a gimmick to make money. There were many Sheiks in wrestling, going back to some of the earliest days of the business. Ali Baba was one of the first. In 1936, he defeated Dick Shikat for one of the two NWA titles in Detroit, a city the "Sheik" Ed Farhat kept alive through the 1970s.

"Wild Bull" Curry was actually a U.S. star with Lebanese lineage. His attitude could instigate a riot at the drop of a hat. He began boxing and wrestling at the age of 14 in carnivals when he brought into the pro ranks. Shortly after World War II, the "Bull" won a world title by defeating Skandor Szabo. Later, he had a main event war at Madison Square Garden with Antonino Rocca that

Sheik Adnan in a match with Mad Dog Vachon.

was out-of-control mayhem. Ironically, when Curry settled down in Connecticut, he worked in law enforcement. His son, "Flying" Fred Curry, worked the Ohio and Michigan areas for promoter Pedro Martinez. The son was talented and charismatic, but never went on to achieve major stardom.

Adnan Al-Kaissey and Kozroh Vasari (The Iron Sheik) are two Middle-Eastern wrestlers with backgrounds as sheiks and amateur stand-outs. Vasari represented Iran in the 1968 Mexico City Olympic Games and Al-

From a cartoon strip to the ring went this tiger

Tiger Mask was the first commercially popular wrestling star in Japan. The original, Satoru Sayama, dazzled crowds with his never-before-seen high-flying moves in the late 1970s and early 1980s. Cartoon series, action figures, and masks were a popular accompaniment to the wrestler who was a favorite with children. Since Sayama donned the mask, two more Japanese wrestlers have extended the character's life span. Through www.highspots.com, fans can purchase these delightful masks even today for around $100. The wrestling mask is a popular item in Mexico and Japan, with Thunder Liger, Rey Mysterio, and Tiger Mask among the most collectible.

Kaissey went to Oklahoma State on a football scholarship but wound up a heavyweight wrestler and AAU champion.

"When I look back, I can't believe what I did," recalled Al-Kaissey. "When they said football, I thought it was (American) soccer. All we did as kids in Baghdad was wrestle and play soccer. I never even heard of the term 'pigskin'."

Al-Kaissey worked hard to become a football player, but he is proudest of his wrestling. "The guy could go forever," said friend and fellow trainer Eddie Sharkey. "They say Adnan was one of the best. Danny Hodge admitted to me he was glad he never had to get in the ring with Adnan."

Kaissey first heard cheers in his career in Portland as a Native American named Billy White Wolf. He returned to Iraq for almost seven years before coming back to the States as the Sheik, where he performed in the AWA and became a legend. Both he and Vasari became hated men in wrestling. The Iron Sheik won the WWF world title by defeating Bob Backlund at the Garden in New York and Al-Kaissey later led Sgt. Slaughter to the WWF gold as a manager named General Adnan.

General Skandor Akbar wasn't from the Middle East, but played the part. He didn't even try to speak Arabic, but with oddities like the One Man Gang and Kimala, he was a featured manager in Dallas' World Class organization. Others, like Al-Kaissey, were real and fierce.

Perhaps most

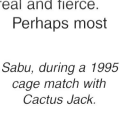

Sabu, during a 1995 cage match with Cactus Jack.

Sabu and Onita promoting their feud in XPW.

famous of all is Detroit's Sheik, Ed Farhat. Born of Lebanese heritage, Farhat began grappling in the late 1940s. He continued to slice and dice foes in Japan at an age when many others had long since put their boots to rest. Oddly, he and real-life nephew Terry Brunk (Sabu) seemed to imitate a person from India rather than the Arab nations. By dropping the "Araby" from the moniker he used early in his career and instilling pure mayhem into his arsenal, the Sheik became a powerful headliner in the U.S. and Canada in the 1950s. By the 1960s and 1970s, he truly evolved into a legend.

Sheik regularly headlined Toronto's Maple Leaf Gardens, Detroit's Cobo Hall, and the well-respected St. Louis Kiel Auditorium. He would maim himself and opponents' foreheads, shoulders, and arms with gashes from a fork or razor blade. Nobody was safe from the Sheik's apparent terror. His feuds with Bobo Brazil, Dusty Rhodes, and Terry Funk carried throughout the U.S. and eventually Japan. In Japan, the Sheik and partner Tiger Jeet Singh became maestros in blood. By the 1970s, Sheik wore out his welcome in Detroit, as crowds dwindled from 12,000 to 1,200. But as long as he was willing to wreak havoc on himself and others, Sheik was always welcome in Japan.

Stars from the Indian nations

Singh is a name in India more commonly used than Smith in the U.S. It has religious overtones and has been around since the country's inception. Few wrestlers from India have ventured outside their homeland. Lance Von Erich, Johnny Powers, and a few others have been successful in South America. But few of the local heroes travel far. One who dared to cross the waters was Singh.

In South Africa and India, Tiger Jeet Singh and Dana Singh were the top draws in the 1960s and 1970s. Later on, Gama Singh hit U.S. rings. But Tiger made the biggest impact of them all. In Japan, he had blood-baths against the Sheik and Inoki. Brute force and guaranteed blood were his calling cards. Tiger, like the Sheik, was active into the 1990s when he helped usher in a decade of decadence for Atsushi Onita's Frontier Martial Arts promotion. For most of his career, he would have to have been considered one of the top 100 stars in wrestling.

A nephew, Tiger Ali Singh, has been trying to make his name in the WWF. The bearded, turban-wearing Ali is bigger and stronger than Tiger and may evolve nicely into a mid-level performer. Lately, Singh has been managing the tag team of Chaz and D-Lo Brown.

Europeans bring their proper skills to the U.S.

Stars from Europe have made their presence felt in U.S. rings as well. Frank Anderson had all the goods. He was 6-foot-

Mil Mascaras in a still shot from the movie, "Los Campeones Justicieros." Mascaras was an international draw in the 1970s.

5, 275 pounds, was a martial artist, and trained with technical wizard, Brad Rheingans. Anderson toured small independents to learn his craft and appeared to be the next superstar. Then, after he failed in WCW, he went back to Sweden never to be heard from again. Tony Halme was another performer pegged for stardom. The large Halme faired well in New Japan Pro Wrestling. Although he is still active as a pro boxer, he failed in the U.S. as a wrestler. In the WWF, fans ran for the concession stands when his character, Ludvig Borga, entered the ring in the 1990s.

The real-life Italian heritage of many wrestlers was in turn used as a popular gimmick beginning in the 1950s. It was used heavily on the East Coast. Of course, Bruno

No holds barred action overseas

Fans in North America are generally not aware of the volume of collectibles that are produced in Japan, but wrestling is hugely popular in Japan and often its stars become national heroes. While Frontier Martial Arts Wrestling would never be confused with the mainstream groups there, the promotion has a loyal following for the brutal and bloody matches it promotes. Stars like Masato Tanaka and Hayabusa regularly appear there. Trading cards such as these are familiar items in Japan and most groups have entire sets made on their behalf. They are not available in the U.S., but for that reason, die-hard collectors have found ways to buy them. The sets usually will be found for $40.

Sammartino was the greatest Italian draw of all-time. Other Italian-born wrestlers were Gino Brito (Canadian-Italian), Tony Parisi (Antonio Pugliese), Dom DeNucci (WWF star who trained Mick Foley), and the Sicilians, Tony Altamore and Lou Albano. Tony Marino (Batman) and Gary Quaterenelli (Italian Stallion in the 1980s) had regional success but just didn't make big names for themselves. Salvatore Bellomo was a brief hit in the 1980s and had numerous WWF stints, but never really made an adequate living from the ring. Little Guido is saddled with a quirky gimmick in ECW, but make no mistake, Guido is one of today's pure wrestlers. Johnny the Bull, Big Vito, and Disco Inferno have shown a glimpse of excellence with WCW and use their Italian heritage as a badge of honor.

Japanese figures elusive, but great find

Japanese fans have always taken to foreign wrestlers. Terry Funk, Hulk Hogan, Big Van Vader, Stan Hansen, Bruiser Brody, and Dr. Death Steve Williams are just some of the stars who have been embraced through the years. Collectors at heart, the Japanese released a Super Pro Wrestler Series of action figures that featured two more of their favorites, Abdullah the Butcher and Andre the Giant. Difficult to obtain in the U.S., these dolls have been seen selling in their original packaging for more than $100 each through an Internet auction.

It takes a masked star to overcome vampires like these

During the 1970s, fans of Mexico's Lucha Libre professional wrestling were given a treat. Their favorite stars were alive and kicking not only in the ring, but on the movie screen. National icons El Santo and Mil Mascaras starred in countless campy thrillers where the evil entity they were chasing was more than a rudo, or bad guy, wrestler. In the films, they fought vampires, mummies and monsters. These promotional photographs from a 1970s film, titled, "Los Vampiros de Coyoacan" starred Mascaras and Superzan. Today, the films are sought-after by collectors for their nostalgia. They are also part of a genre of movie all to their own. Promo items can be found in movie shops in Hollywood. These pictures were recently available for $75. The movies are also available, although without English subtitles, for around $30.

Chapter 8

Managers: The Folks Fans Love to Hate

Managers have always been a vital part of professional wrestling. In the early years, Farmer Burns served as Frank Gotch's manager. Burns not only trained Gotch—much in the manner of a drill instructor—but he also helped secure the proper sparring partners and fights for the wrestler. Burns' main job was to finesse the media and be Gotch's mouthpiece.

In later years, managers changed. No longer were they legitimate handlers of a wrestler's affairs; now they were every bit a part of the show as the ring warriors. In time, managers became exceptional, if not essential, players in a wrestling territory.

Like wrestlers, managers come in all shapes and sizes. A large percentage of them was traditional heat seekers whose job was to rile up the masses by putting down the babyfaces. Not all, though: A few, like Arnold Skaaland (who managed Bruno Sammartino and Bob Backlund) played it straight down the middle as an honest Joe. Others, like Tommy Gilbert, Eddie Marlin, Paul Ellering, and Jackie Fargo were corner men of the fan favorites. While useful, these types of managers were no more than glorified cheerleaders. Aside from Skaaland and Burns, few managers made a national impact by helping a good guy. Ideally, hometown heroes don't need help getting cheered. After all, their foes should be so despicable that figuring out who fans should root for becomes a simple, clean-cut decision. Instead, managers were, and still are, attached to the heels.

There have been just a few categories of managers. One is the former wrestlers who turned to managing because they were either too injured or old to perform in the ring. Another group are the folks who were essentially fans who got a chance to break the inner circle of wrestling and become a character themselves. The ones that fall into this group like James E. Cornette (who was first a ring photographer), Paul Heyman (who contributed to wrestling magazines), the late Mark Curtis (Brian Hildebrand), and Professor Steve Druk, were generally very good, if not exceptional, managers.

As storylines explain, managers have always been the sleaziest characters on a show. They have a propensity toward cheating and always complain

The Brain Trust: Freddie Blassie, Lou Albano, the Grand Wizard, and Oliver Humperdink.

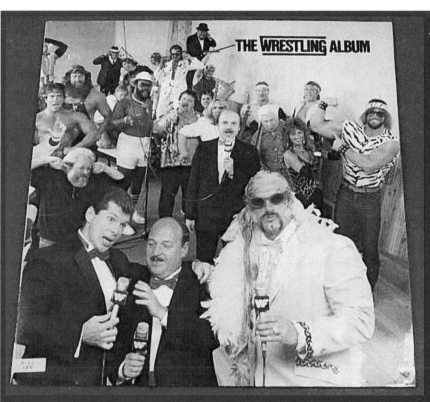

about lack of microphone time, but they usually have a great sense of humor. A good manager could actually make a territory; a great one could provide sell-outs.

Young fans traditionally hate all managers. But as we get older, we've learned to appreciate the intricacies of their excellence. "Wild" Red Berry was one of the first heel managers. Just Berry's presence alone was enough to guarantee that his team, The Fabulous Kangaroos, would be jeered. As territories regionalized through local television outlets, managers became essential parts to the promoting puzzle. Sam Bass roughed-up folks in Memphis, "Crybaby" George Cannon bullied foes in Detroit, Tarzan Tyler plagued the Rougeau family in Montreal, Eddie Creechman was a soul mate of the Sheik in Detroit, and King Curtis bled throughout Hawaii. In the 1950s and '60s, managers became part of the show—a big part.

Classic heels

The 1970s and 1980s were the glory years for managers and the WWF, during that time, was a haven for them. The insanely aloof Captain Lou Albano, former wrestler Classy Freddy Blassie, and the eccentric Grand Wizard were mainstays there as heel managers. They all guided champions at one time. It was the Wizard who helped dethrone championship icons like Bruno Sammartino, Pedro Morales, and "Superstar" Billy Graham. Albano will be the first to tell anyone within earshot that he managed 17 tag-team champions while in the WWF. With Tony Altamore, the Captain himself was part of a moderately successful team, the Sicilians. Rather than retire, though, Albano became a mastermind of tag teams.

Albano was beyond weird. He loved Hawaiian-style, short-sleeve shirts, he wore rubber bands on his face, and he was not afraid to get beat up or bleed. His booming, bizarre voice didn't hurt his image, either. One of the most successful teams Albano

Grand Wizard with a blonde Ken Patera.

Capt. Lou Albano and Blondie lead singer Debbie Harry.

managed was the Valiant Brothers. The three men who made up the team weren't much before promoters stuck them with Albano. "Luscious" Johnny Valentine was a floundering veteran, Jerry Valiant was a noted mid-level performer who was considered a good person to have in the locker room, and "Handsome" Jimmy Valiant was young and had a rock- 'n'-roll feel. The three blondes even made a record. The Valiants' trademark was the long wrestling trunks they wore with catch phrases written on them. Without Albano, the threesome probably would have faded away into obscurity; with the Captain, however, they became a famed team.

Albano became something of a caricature of himself in the 1990s. While riding on his

Another king has his way in Memphis

What else would you expect from a wrestler named the King? Jerry Lawler, a Memphis icon for 30 years, has always embraced Elvis Presley, so it came as no surprise when he released his compact disc titled "Memphis' Other King." Through the years, Lawler has used several of his own tunes as ring entrance music. On this disc, fans will find 16 tracks including "Trouble," which was used as the soundtrack for one of Lawler's music videos, "Brown-Eyed Girl," and "Bad News." It can be purchased through Lawler's website at www.kinglawler.com for $15. Many wrestlers, like Jimmy Valiant, Jim Brunzell, and the Crusher, have released singles, but Lawler's record stands above the pack.

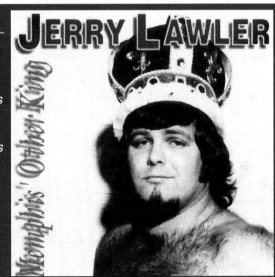

The application form (image at top left):

STATE OF NEW YORK
DEPARTMENT OF STATE
DIVISION OF
STATE ATHLETIC COMMISSION

THIS SPACE FOR
COMMISSION USE ONLY

Chapter 714, Laws of 1921

APPLICATION FOR
WRESTLER'S LICENSE

Fee $5.00

The undersigned having paid the legal fee as provided in Chapter 714 of the Laws of 1921, hereby makes application for a License as a Wrestler.

Name *Louis J. Albano*   Date *Aug. 4, 1958*
Ring Name *Lou Albano*
Address ... *N.Y. Verner* State *New York*
Age *25*   Date of Birth *July 5, 1933*   Place of Birth *Rome, Italy*

PROOF OF AGE
Birth Certificate *Rome* School Record *High School* Baptismal Certificate *St. Peter* Passport...
Any Official Document Showing Birth Date...
Normal Weight *250*   Ring Weight *240*   Color *W*
Married *Yes*   Single   Citizen *Yes*
Occupation *Delicatessen Worker*
Employees name and address...
References... Address... Address... Address...

Have you ever been convicted of a crime? *no*
If so, when and where? Give full particulars...

Name and address of manager *Manhattan Wrestling Enterprise*
Is manager authorized to contract for your appearance or services? *Yes*

The Commission must be notified promptly of any change in manager or terms of contract with manager, and failure to so notify the Commission may result in the suspension or revocation of this license.

(OVER)

Did he get a license for the rubber bands?

Before professional wrestling was de-regulated in numerous states, the wrestlers were required to be licensed. New Jersey and New York were two states with known wrestling and boxing commissions. This 1950s wrestling license application was submitted by Lou Albano in New York. In 1954, Albano applied with the New York State Athletic Commission and the wrestler-to-be paid $5 to receive his license. Items such as this are highly collectible and amazingly can be found for sale through different outlets. Estate sales or private collections, which are unloaded in auctions, are generally the ideal place to find one-of-a-kind items such as this.

laurels after his cameo in Cyndi Lauper's smash video hit, "Girls Just Want to Have Fun," his creative juices seemed to be drained. He did get up for one more run in the WWF with the popular British Bulldogs, but by the 1990s, he was semi-retired.

When Albano was on top, few could generate heat, or jeers, like the Captain. When he pressured good guy Jimmy Snuka into jilting the fans, Albano became a super heel. In the storylines, when Snuka realized Albano was a bigger hindrance than help, the muscular islander turned on Albano and became a wildly popular babyface. Without Albano as the foil, no matter how great Snuka was, he would have never attained such fan worship if it were not for Albano.

Fred Blassie was much of the same. He knew exactly when to call a fan favorite a "pencil-necked geek" and even recorded a song by that title. He had the looks of a movie-star heel and even appeared in various television programs. He could baffle crowds with words only scholars knew and could get down and dirty with the best of them. Any time Blassie was around, money

Lou Albano and wrestling fan Andy Kaufman.

was to be made. The last team he managed to stardom was Nikolai Volkoff and Iron Sheik in the late 1980s.

While Albano, Blassie, and the Grand Wizard reigned in the WWF in the 1970s, a young and talented Bobby "The Brain" Heenan was juggling his schedule between the AWA and Dick the Bruiser's WWA in Indianapolis. The eloquent Nick Bockwinkel, who Heenan later managed, gave Heenan the nickname "The Brain." But fans preferred to call him the "Weasel." In fact, Heenan once lost a series of matches against the Rock & Roll Buck Zumhoff and was forced to wear a weasel suit each time he lost.

Heenan fit like a glove with Bockwinkel, the AWA world champion. While the classy champion teetered on earning the fans' respect, Heenan's taunts would never fail to push the fans over the edge and hate Bockwinkel even more. At times, Heenan was so sharp and so witty, his work would carry an entire AWA television program. He continued to drive AWA fans crazy until the 1980s, when he joined the WWF.

After managing the greats in the AWA like the Blackjacks, Pat Patterson, and Ray Stevens, Heenan was more than ready to part for the new nationally acclaimed group.

Gordon Solie interviews Bobby "The Brain" Heenan and The Superstar.

Heenan was right at home in the WWF. At first, he managed Jesse Ventura, Big John Studd and years later, Ric Flair and Rick Rude. He also broke new ground with his job as a heel commentator. With his television partner, the late Gorilla Monsoon, Heenan was almost like a Vaudeville act. Heenan's array of one-liners tapped into Monsoon's role as a straight man. But when they worked together, there was undeniable magic. Heenan played the perfect buffoon at times and was never afraid to be the butt of a joke. The Brain left the WWF in the mid-1990s for promises of a bigger paycheck and greener pastures to be part of the WCW's team of announcers. As hard as he tried, even Heenan couldn't help the WCW.

Bobby Heenan was once a decent wrestler, too. Here he battles Art Thomas.

Ex-wrestlers Paul Jones, Sonny King, and Paul Ellering gave serviceable performances on Georgia Championship Wrestling. But they were no match for the young and enthusiastic Michael Hayes and Roddy Piper. Hayes wrestled and managed and his team, the Freebirds, brought wrestling into new areas of skill. Piper, after ring wars with Greg Valentine and Flair, was given a reprieve from ring action and was allowed to announce with the late Gordon Solie. To settle feuds for him, he recruited the one and only Abdullah. With that combination, a foundation for mayhem was laid.

In the 1980s, it was Ole Anderson, J.J. Dillon, and Jim Cornette who grabbed the headlines. Cornette is one person who bleeds wrestling. He entered the business as a writer/photographer and some of the pictures in this book are pictures that he shot as a youth in Memphis and Louisville. After paying his dues as a photographer, Cornette

An older Jim Cornette with Midnight Express.

was ready for prime time on camera. He began managing in Memphis and did some of his best work there. Later, for Bill Watts' Mid-South Promotion, Cornette managed the Midnight Express, a team that gave him the most national exposure. The team went to Dallas for a short time and then hit it big in Georgia for Jim Crockett's NWA on WTBS. In the mid-1990s, Cornette made his way to the WWF, where he guided Yokozuna, Owen Hart, and Big Van Vader. Today, after 25 years in the business, he oversees Ohio Valley Wrestling, a feeder group for the WWF.

Over the years, Cornette was at his best with wrestlers who could perform in the ring, but were not known as having interview skills. Without Cornette's mile-a-minute promises and threats, his polyester suit, and trademark tennis racquet, Dennis Condrey, Bobby Eaton, and Stan Lane may never have made it past the mid-card status they were in when Cornette found them. Today,

A very young Jim Cornette.

Oliver Humperdink, right, with Lord Humongous.

the Midnight Express is widely seen as the best tag-team ever.

Other managers, while not major factors nationally, were solid regional acts. "Playboy" Gary Hart dedicated his life to ruining the life of Dusty Rhodes in Florida. Hart tried to run him out of the Sunshine State with the Asian Assassins and Dirty Dick Slater. He even convinced babyface Bob Roop to face Big Dusty. But no one could get the job done. Hart spent most of the 1980s in World Class in Dallas with Abdullah the Butcher and again with Kabuki. He also had a run in the NWA with Al Perez and the Great Muta. Oliver Humperdink had a brief run in the WWF in the 1980s with Bam Bam Bigelow as his main charge. A lifelong fan, the flashy Humperdink wreaked havoc in Florida during the 1970s and 1980s. He partnered with a crazed Kevin Sullivan to form a satanic-like wrestling family. It was a host of oddities with only once common goal: ridding the area of Rhodes.

As Hart was fading into history, a young Paul E. Dangerously was making a name for himself in the East. Bold, brash, and carrying a cell phone, Dangerously was the epitome of the new breed of managers. He payed homage to the greats while never usurping his crew and he was willing to do whatever it took to help a promoter (like losing his hair in a cage match and managing three times in one night for a measly $85).

As a 12-year-old, Dangerously took pictures for Vince McMahon Sr. in the WWF. By his 20s, he turned his attention to becoming an on-air personality and eventually was managing nationally in Memphis, the AWA, and later WCW. In the early '90s, he returned to the East Coast. He decided to take himself away from television storylines and instead worked behind-the-scenes in ECW. In his 10-year managing career, he was in the corner of the Original Midnight Express (Dennis Condrey and Randy Rose), Jack Victory, Eddie Gilbert, Mean Mark (The Undertaker), The Dangerous Alliance (Bobby Eaton & Arn Anderson), Tommy Rich, Austin Idol, and many others. He was meticulous, loud, and respectful of the business—that made him one of the true greats to circle ringside.

Managers always had a life of their own, and fans were never sure where these characters came from. Slick, once a Kansas City street preacher who was friends with Bruiser Brody, was a big name for the WWF in the 1980s. Donning a turban as a sheik was always a big way to become a manager and Skandor Akbar and Adnan Al Kaissey were two of the finest.

Of late, managing is a lost art. Wrestlers today realize they need to talk on camera themselves, if they want to win over fans, and slowly, managers have become extra bodies that promotions don't need. This has been a trend through the 1990s. Robert Fuller, Sonny Onoo, and Wally Yamaguchi had runs in the WWF and WCW, but not for long. Jimmy Hart got lost in the shuffle in WCW. Bill Alphonso became a cheerleader for Tazz, Rob Van Dam, and Sabu in ECW. Sunny (Tammy Sytch) was a star, but faded quickly once away from the WWF, and Sal E. Graziano has not been a sizable factor in ECW. Even the usually dramatic Hayes took a lesser role with the Hardy Boys and Raven managed a flock for a short time. Let's hope that this important piece of wrestling lore is not lost forever.

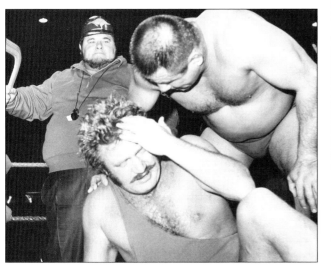

George "Crybaby" Cannon, called one of the world's greatest wrestling managers, puts the finishing touches to Pepper Gomez and Red Bastien after "The Fabulous Kangaroos" victory.

Manager Jimmy Hart, the "Mouth of the South."

Larry Sharpe, manager of Bam Bam Bigelow.

Jerry Jarrett and Tojo Yamamoto.

At its annual convention in 1978, the National Wrestling Alliance presented a plaque to promoter Sam Muchnick in appreciation for his many years of service to both the NWA and wrestling in general.

General Skandor Akbar and the One Man Gang.

Hotstuff Eddie Gilbert.

A young Vince McMahon interviews an animated Grand Wizard.

ECW manager Fonzie.

Trainer of the stars Eddie Sharkey.

Minneapolis promoter Wally Karbo.

Chapter 9

The Ring Beauties

Female wrestlers have always had the cards stacked against them. Their history in professional wrestling goes back many years, but women have always had a difficult time attaining prominence in this male-dominated business.

Traditionally, women were never really allowed the golden opportunity to work in a feud to their fullest potential. Promoters mainly limited women to one singles or tag-team match—and they were

Penny Banner.

lucky to get that. In the United States, female wrestlers have mostly been used as special attractions.

Former NWA champion Ric Flair got to wrestle thousands of all-star performers the world over. He worked programs (feuds) with the best of the best. Rightfully, Flair deserved his spot and he made the best of his opportunities. But like all males, if Flair had failed to become a star, he would have had no one to blame but himself.

It can be assumed that Flair probably wrestled more main-event matches in one year than renowned women's champion Wendi Richter wrestled in her entire career. To become a top female wrestler in the U.S., she had to be special—extra special. It would be unfair to compare the differences of men in the ring to that of what women, when properly trained, can offer. The line of thinking was that women should only be used on occasion. But while all promotions were loaded with male talent, when promoters needed a special, annual draw to attract fans, they would think nothing of calling in one of the "girls."

There were less than 100 experienced women wrestlers in the U.S. during the 1980s. As for men, it's realistic to believe there were as many as 2,000, with nearly

June Byers, world-championship wrestler.

Donna Christanello rides piggy back on Fabulous Moolah, while Kathy O'Day dishes out a few rough bumps for Toni Rose—but Moolah and Rose took two out of three falls in this match from the 1970s.

500 making a considerable living. About a dozen women actually made enough money to be full-time performers. Women may have wanted to "just have fun," as singer Cyndi Lauper crooned, but when it came to wrestling, opportunities for women and their families were few.

Up until the 1960s, some states even outlawed women's wrestling. But as the years passed, females fought the odds and became the favorites of many fans. Whether it is the Fabulous Moolah, Joyce Grable, Betty Nicolai, Princess Little Cloud, Susan Green, Richter, or Molly Holly and Lita, all women deserve an H—as in heroine—next to their name in the wrestling history books.

Today, women play prominent roles in wrestling. Take the WWF's Chyna. She has become wrestling's true barrier-breaking star. Beautiful enough to pose for *Playboy Magazine* and brawny enough to hold the men's Intercontinental title, the woman nicknamed the "Ninth Wonder of the World" has proven to be a star for the ages.

Police Gazette, a now-defunct magazine that rated wrestlers, recognized Alice Williams to be the first women's champion. The queen of carnival wrestling was recognized as champ through the turn of the 20th Century, but faded into obscurity as wrestling ventured into larger stadiums and arenas. Long before Chyna lit up television screens, the first woman of prominence was Mildred Burke. Burke took women's

wrestling out of the sideshow that Williams was stuck in. Born Mildred Bliss of Coffeyville, Kansas, Burke spent hours grooming movie-star looks and carried herself like a champion. She held major titles from 1936 through her retirement in the late 1950s. She also trained and promoted her own stable of superstars until she passed away in 1988 at age 73.

Vivian Vachon will be remembered as one of wrestling's top female stars. In an era

Marty O'Neill interviews Butcher Vachon and Vivian Vachon in the 1960s.

A singing Vivian Vachon in the recording studio.

Chyna is one of the most prominent women wrestlers in the ring today.

Tag-team champs, Lelani Kai and Fabulous Moolah.

when wrestling women were oddities to say the least, she was a very talented wrestler. Born and raised in Montreal, Vachon was the sister of the legendary Mad Dog (Maurice) and Butcher (Paul) Vachon. She started wrestling at the age of 20 and toured all around the U.S. and also Japan and Australia. Although she never dethroned the great Fabulous Moolah, few females could compete at her level. Vachon was also a crossover star. Her French-Canadian albums sold well in Canada and Europe and she took both her singing and wrestling very seriously. Vachon was a featured performer in the film, "The Wrestling Queen," a 1980s documentary still available on video. Sadly, she and her daughter Julie were killed in a 1991 auto accident in Montreal.

Fearsome and fabulous

Few wrestlers—both female and male— have the credentials of Lillian Ellison. As "Slave Girl Moolah," Ellison became a top-drawing valet, and later a wrestler, in the

1930s. It wasn't until she changed her name to the Fabulous Moolah that Ellison first won a world title. In the years that her career progressed, Moolah was to women's wrestling what the great Jackie Robinson was to baseball. During Moolah's time, the majority of tightly knit promoters in the 1930s and 1950s had little time to put women in the ring. Even the male wrestlers themselves felt that women would take away their thunder. Men were threatened to say the least. Wisely, Moolah eased into the ranks first as a valet. It seemed that a valet named Slave Girl threatened few and actually added appeal to the show.

When Moolah took to wrestling full-time, her physical toughness and ability earned her respect. Even as a title holder, Moolah rarely could settle into a territory to work a feud for any extended amount of time. "Have tights, will travel" became her mantra. She crisscrossed the world fanatically without tiring. After years of wanting to join the WWF, promoters finally gave Moolah her shot. So, in 1956 in Baltimore, Moolah beat Judy Grable and won her first WWF title. Amazingly, Moolah held that title for 28 years over the course of four decades. With New York's Madison Square Garden the home base of the WWF, Moolah fought the state's law that had prohibited women from wrestling professionally. After years of haggling with the New York State Athletic Commission, she was finally allowed to perform at the Garden in the 1960s. She stayed with the WWF until the 1980s.

Wendi Richter holds one of the many belts she won during her career.

In 1984, a young and pretty girl named Wendi Richter defeated Moolah to win the belt and ended the fabulous one's reign. At the time, Richter was at the top of her game so promoters gave her a shot. Richter was part of the WWF's first media explosion. While she held the belt, she was immensely popular. She can thank the legendary feud with Lou Albano for that. Vince McMahon linked Richter with pop star Lauper and the feud spilled over to the first Wrestlemania. Richter's exposure on MTV gave her the attention that women had long searched for. Truly, it was a unique time for Richter. Although women were not main attractions after that, the WWF did give some females an opportunity to shine. In the years that followed, Sherri Martel, Rockin' Robin Smith, Velvet McIntyre, Alundra Blaze (Madusa Micelli), and Lelani Kai held the belt until around 1990, when it simply disappeared.

Beauties from afar

Over in Japan, the 1980s championed a new breed of women wrestlers. The sport there had a very special blend of fast action, high-risk maneuvers and an edgy, bloody, hardcore style. Women like Chigusa Nagayo became pop icons, appearing in highly rated television shows and singing pop songs.

Promoters in Japan have made it a tradition to give their biggest ring stars recording deals for extra merchandising. The phenomenon worked, as arenas were packed and crowds went nuts for their favorites. Several women from Japan used their momentum gained in their homeland in the U.S. The Jumping Bomb Angels (Itsuki Yamazaki and Noriyo Tateno) once held the WWF's women's tag-team titles during a feud with the Glamour Girls.

Other stars in Japan were born out of the new style. Dump Matsumoto, Devil Masami, Aja Kong, and Bull Nakano even had their own styles that blended the Road Warriors' ring presence with the intensity of Bruiser Brody and Stan Hansen.

Masami was a pure screamer (far before Daphne) and Lioness Asuka, Akiro Hokuto, Manami Toyota, and Cutie Suzuki gave stellar performances. No one had quite seen women perform at this level before, as some of the most compelling matches of any kind were held during this time. After this boom period, women's wrestling in Japan slowed. When a wrestler was at her peak physically at age 25, she was forced to quit to make room for new talent. This led to some of the women to start their own rival promotions and circumvent the archaic rules, but fans wanted little part in a watered-down product. After being acclimated to the greatest women's wrestling ever, fans just went away.

Other women of note

In the U.S., women always played second fiddle to the Japanese. Promoter David McLane had a vision in the 1980s to exclusively promote women's wrestling (Gorgeous Ladies of Wrestling, Powerful Women of Wrestling) and Tor Berg tried it with the Ladies

Japanese women's star Akira Hokuto.

Sherri Martel, in her days as a wrestler.

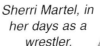

After she hung up her tights as a wrestler, Sherri Martel went on to become known as the greatest women's manager ever.

afraid to take a fall from high places. Even though her job was at ringside, Martel worked the match at a pace that most men would not keep even in the ring. Martel went on to WCW during the early 1990s and finished her career as a manager for then-hells Harlem Heat.

Another woman to emerge from the AWA was Debbie Micelli. Once a nurse's aide, Micelli found a spot for herself when Martel left for the WWF. Micelli, nicknamed Madusa, managed Nick Kiniski and Kevin Kelly, as well as Curt Hennig for a short time. But Micelli had been taught how to wrestle and she did not see herself solely as eye candy, so she practiced and trained and actually became quite a wrestler. In the 1980s, opportunity knocked again. The promoters in Japan wanted the blond-haired maven to come to their country and feud with Nagayo. Madusa packed her bags and matured as a star. While in Japan, Madusa won championships, feuded with Nagayo, and also recorded an album. She is a true devotee of the sport and was once wedded to Greg Valentine. When her Japan tour was over, Madusa returned to the U.S. and started in the WWF as Alundra Blaze, eventually winning the title. She changed groups again and left for WCW, where she toiled as both a valet and wrestler. Generally, wherever she went, Madusa was a top star. But the lack of true competitors in the States prevented Madusa from becoming a bigger star in America.

Since Madusa, the number of true women's

Lita, one of the most popular women in wrestling today.

Professional Wrestling Association. Though nationally syndicated, the groups never caught fire. Of late, McLane is trying again with Women of Wrestling, to limited success.

Some women, though, caught on. Before her time in the WWF as a manager, Sherri Martel was an AWA champion and accomplished performer. In the late 1980s, Martel's role was expanded to manage perennial losers Doug Somers and Buddy Rose. The combination worked and Martel was soon in main events. Rose and Somers had a classic feud with the Midnight Rockers (Shawn Michaels and Marty Janetty) and Martel continued to wrestle. She was very good at generating jeers from the crowd. Vince McMahon took notice and Martel was soon headed for greener pastures. In the WWF, Martel managed Randy Savage and later Michaels. As a manager, Martel, now coined Scary Sherri by her opposition, was incredible. Not many, if any, women were as adept as her at causing trouble. Martel was not wrestlers has decreased. Of late, the WWF has a monopoly on most of the marketable female wrestlers. The group is not only a place for beautiful valets: Ivory, Molly Holly, Jackie, Torri, and Lita are all trained professionals. Molly is one of the more underrated talents. As Miss Mona in WCW, she was a balanced technician, but like many before her, lacked competition. In the WWF, Molly has shown she can wrestle and be an entertaining personality as the storyline cousin of Crash and Bob Holly. Ivory, meanwhile, has wrestled for numerous all-women's groups during the past 12 years and was more than deserving of her recent WWF opportunity. She is one of the veterans now with a true wrestling background and does amazingly well in interviews. Jackie, the former Miss Texas, is sexy and witty. Like Ivory, she is a well trained wrestler having battled in the USWA in Memphis. Of late, Lita has shown flashes of brilliance. She was trained by her real-life beau, Matt Hardy, and takes a page out of his book with flying moves that would make a circus performer proud. The Kat (Miss Kitty) is another WWF talent, but is not trained as a wrestler. Though she may have a voyeuristic side, she has been around for several years gaining experience in Memphis and is never afraid of mixing it up in the ring.

The valets: Puppies, cigars, and plastic surgery

The Fabulous Moolah began her career as a valet. But through the 1940s, there were women who only accompanied men to the ring. "The Human Orchid" Gorgeous George changed everything.

Using his real name, George Wager was a mid-level performer. Then, he changed his ring name to Gorgeous George and hired his wife, Betty, to appear with him. She would primp his hair and spray perfume in the air. The act was a success and promoters, who were taking advantage of television

for the first time, were sold on the idea of valets.

Ring valets have become a staple in wrestling. Even so, there have been cycles of popularity for valets. Some women have made entire careers from coming to the ring with men. Miss Linda was never far from the wild Adrian Street, and Brenda Britton seemed to be joined at the hip of "Hustler" Rip Rogers. Both Street and Rogers were territorial stars through the 1970s. In the mid-1980s, the World Class area caught fire with a bevy of beauties. Raven Rude, Sunshine, Baby Doll, and Precious added new enthusiasm to the company's already-explosive television program. Prior to hooking up with Precious, Jimmy Garvin was just another average wrestler chugging away. With Precious, Garvin rejuvenated his career himself and became the ire of many male fans. The petite blond played the part well and knew how to generate heat at ringside.

The Universal Wrestling Federation utilized the incredible beauty of Missy Hyatt, who was the valet of Eddie Gilbert in his group, Hot Stuff International. Her valley-girl interviews and floosie appearance were a hit. After her stay in the UWF, she played her

Macho Man Randy Savage impresses Miss Elizabeth by ripping up a photo of Bruno Sammartino.

career's most prominent role in the NWA and WCW as a television personality. Later on, Hyatt even had a try-out with the WWF as a talk-show hostess. Visually, Missy had great appeal and in many ways set the stage for today's glitzy females.

The WWF had its own women in the 1980s. Miss Elizabeth played the damsel in distress in textbook fashion as the valet for her ex-husband, Randy Savage. She originally met Savage in the Tennessee area in the early 1980s. Savage was the champion of an outlaw promotion, while Liz was a weather caster at a local television station. When they met, it set in motion a top attraction. Liz was by Macho Man's side during his epic battles at Wrestlemanias and Saturday Night's Main Event specials. Although she was not a great talker, she was an expert at less-is-more. With her gasps and from covering her face with her hands in distress, she captivated fans. She may have had her detractors, but her 1980s run in the WWF was nothing less than stunning. In the 1990s, she and Savage divorced, but oddly enough, they both found employment in WCW. While there, she was at the side of many wrestlers like Hulk Hogan and Eric Bischoff, but she was always underutilized and never really maintained her momentum from the WWF.

Recently, the WWF has turned up the sex appeal with a new array of valets. Perhaps none was bigger than Reno Mero, the valet formerly known as Sable. She had a short stint in the WWF, but it was nothing short of fantastic. When Sunny left the group in the mid-1990s, Sable, wife of wrestler Marc Mero (Johnny B. Badd) was put in her place. Fans approved. She had great sex appeal and helped usher in the WWF's "Attitude" ad campaign. She was so marketable, Mero was given a cover pictorial in Playboy. At her peak of popularity, she left the WWF and sued for sexual harassment. Actually, her exit from wrestling garnished more publicity than her career itself. After her promise of stardom, she has been virtually unseen during the last two years.

Terri Runnels came from WCW as Alexandra York to manage her then-husband Dustin Rhodes. Runnels played the part of Marlena, while Rhodes wrestled as the unforgettable Goldust. Her pre-Monica Lewinsky cigar antics and sexy taunts gave

Manager Nancy Sullivan, better known as just "Woman."

Manager Francine of the ECW.

the Goldust character an edge. This is one case where a valet was used perfectly. Dustin did his best to make the eerie gimmick work, but Marlena gave the character life. Had it not been for Marlena's devilish charm, Goldust may have been another Isaac Yankem. Later on, she divorced Rhodes but stayed in the WWF. Now she is partners with Perry Saturn and is also pushed as a WWF Diva.

The former Debra McMichael has become a cottage industry since Jerry Lawler nicknamed her assets "puppies." She was married to McMichael while in WCW and claims she was always destined for a role on television. Certainly, she has the looks, but her relationship to McMichael didn't hurt her chances for stardom. She also managed Jeff Jarrett before going to the WWF. That move proved to be worthwhile. She managed Jarrett again and his partner, the late Owen

Hart. Now, her role is diminished, but as Steve Austin's real-life wife, Debra will have a job in the WWF for as long as she wants. Trish Stratus joined the WWF with a huge Internet following from her bodybuilding and modeling career. She probably didn't know what to expect with her foray into wrestling. Her career started slow, but she is trying to learn to wrestle in addition to being a valet. Her time in the WWF has seen her with Test and Albert, as well as in a role as the girlfriend of Vince McMahon.

ECW has always been a hotbed of women. From adult film stars (Jasmine St. Clair, Jenna Jamison) to trained wrestlers (Jazz) to plain old beauties (Beulah, Francine, Dawn Marie) the women have been seen as a boost to the younger male viewer demographic. Francine has been the company's most resilient star. She has man-

Manager Tammy Sytch a.k.a. Sunny.

WWF manager Terri.

aged Shane Douglas and Justin Credible, and has never been afraid to take a chair shot or two. Nancy Sullivan (Woman) also was in ECW in its early days. Tammy Sytch, who once performed as Sunny in the WWF, has been in ECW at different times. In the early '90s, Sytch started in Jim Cornette's Smoky Mountain Wrestling group and caught on quickly as a manager. He got a huge break from the WWF to manage the Body Donnas, a team that included her boyfriend, Chris Candido. After the WWF, Sytch ventured to ECW. Her problems with drug abuse were made public in ECW in late 1998. In a cable television interview, Sytch shocked viewers as she wept and openly talked about her personal life. Even if she does not return to the ring, fans will hardly forget her, as she is still one of the more talked about wrestling females.

WCW has had a revolving door for valets. There have been many names, but few have become major stars. Elizabeth, Martel, and Madusa all had chances to shine. Lately, new names sprout up regularly. Kimberly Page, Daphne, Pamela Paulshock, Ms. Hancock, Ryan Shamrock, Aysa, Torrie Wilson, Major Gunns, Paisley, and Midaja have tried to create a niche for themselves, but to limited success. WCW also branded the Nitro Girls phenomena, but poor management of that group, as well as in-fighting between the women, led to its disbandment last year.

Princess Little Cloud, known as the "Apache Indian Beauty, in the 1960s."

Sweet Georgia Brown wrestled in the 1960s.

Barb Nichols (formerly Joyce Grable) and George Becker, in the 1960s.

Joyce Grable and Vicki Williams with their tag-team belts in the 1960s.

Cora Combs and daughter Debbie Combs were a duo in the 1970s.

Jean Antone, a '60s star.

Tully Blanchard and Baby Doll, in the 1980s, before their big split.

Sunshine wrestled in the 1980s.

Joyce Grable and Princess Little Cloud thrilled fans in the 1960s.

Mae Young, a grappler in the 1960s, and a wrestling bear!

The Artist with his manager, Paisley.

Miss Flower Power, known as the "hippie girl wrestler" in the 1960s.

The former Sable, Rena Mero, signs her WWF action figure.

Nicole Bass dwarfs her competition El Cholo. Bass is so tough she has to wrestle the guys.

Ryan Shamrock shows her
worldly side.

Manager Gorgeous George works
the crowd.

ECW manager Dawn Marie sells
her gimmicks.

Scott Steiner with valet Midajah.

1960s wrestler Diamond Lil and Little Tokyo.

Shane Helms lays a smooch on manager/valet Ryan Shamrock.

Shane Douglas with valet Torrie Wilson.

Strong like a man, but certainly a woman

Chyna's stock has certainly been consistently on the rise. Of late, Chyna has written a new book, If They Only Knew, has been on several television shows, and was also the subject of this comic book by Chaos Comics. The issue sold out, as have many of Chaos' wrestling titles, and is high in demand with new collectors. The issue now sells for $15, but like the wrestler herself, that price will continue to rise in time.

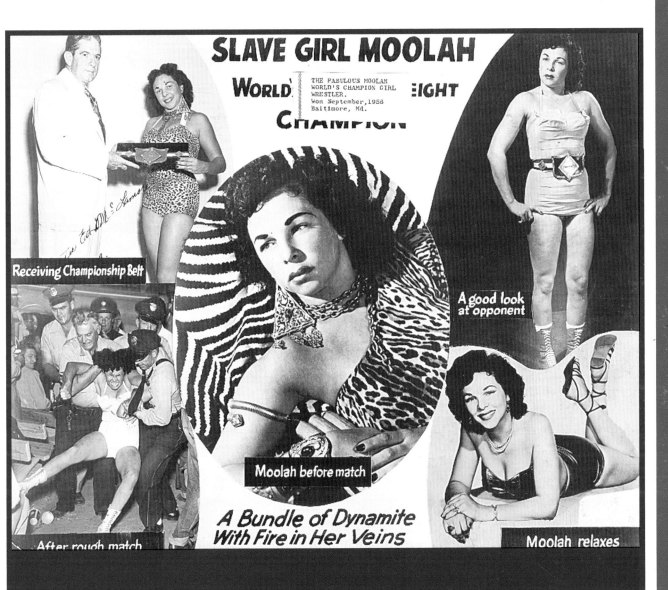

SLAVE GIRL MOOLAH

WORLD'... ...EIGHT

CHAMPION

THE FABULOUS MOOLAH
WORLD'S CHAMPION GIRL
WRESTLER.
Won September,1956
Baltimore, Md.

Receiving Championship Belt

A good look at opponent

Moolah before match

A Bundle of Dynamite With Fire in Her Veins

After rough match

Moolah relaxes

She came a long way, baby

Lillian Ellison was as smart as she was talented. The woman who would later become known worldwide as the Fabulous Moolah had to battle chauvinistic tendencies when she began her career in the 1930s. To work around promoters who were afraid to promote women's wrestling, Ellison worked as a valet under the name Slave Girl Moolah. Later, once she was established, she worked in the ring and had a famous career. As the Slave Girl, Moolah had many fans and a loyal fan-club following. This promotional photo of the Slave Girl was given to fan-club members. On the back, there is a personal letter written from Moolah to one of her fans. The picture with the autograph is worth $125 and shows the value placed on memorabilia from the early days of a champion wrestler's career.

Women were more than a pretty face

Woman wrestlers have always had a unique connection to the sport. They began as ring valets, but quickly moved inside the ring. Mildred Burke and Cora Combs were two wrestlers who had many years of experience between them. This Combs' promo photo explains her days growing up in Hazard, Kentucky. This Burke photograph is a collage of her better moments from the 1950s. Both pictures can be bought for less than $30. More than their value, items like these are important because they trace the lineage of the great women who stepped into the ring.

Sable puts stamp on wrestling

Before Rena Mero left the wrestling industry in 1999, she was an icon in the World Wrestling Federation known as Sable. Mero is the wife of wrestler Marc Mero and reached the top woman's spot in the group in the wake left by Sunny's departure. Mero climbed the ladder of success quickly based on her appearance and even graced the covers of Playboy and TV Guide. Her merchandise became a hot seller. Overseas, and away from United States copyright laws, Sable's image was used on a 1999 stamp. It is one of the few stamps ever to have a wrestling personality on it and is a novelty for ardent sable fans. Through Internet auctions, the stamp can be found for $30.

Chapter 10

Oddballs, Freaks, and Monsters: Gimmicks That Make Wrestling Great

Wrestling wouldn't be much without gimmicks. From the bland to the bizarre and from the mundane to the magnanimous, professional wrestling and promotional gimmicks to get fans interested are seemingly made for one another.

Gimmicks are wrestling's ties to the carnival days when human oddities and human feats of strength were lures to the big tents in small towns everywhere. Promoters would give their pro wrestlers strange names and contrive stories as to their origin. Sometimes, the story was so sensational, legends were born.

Yousouf the Terrible Turk was billed as a

George "The Animal" Steele.

monster from Turkey, who was in North America to take the world's championship back to his homeland: In actuality, the Terrible Turk was from France. Far be it for a wrestling promoter to tell the truth. Tank Abbott, as another example, is a barroom fighter from the Ultimate Fighting circuit, who came to the WCW in 1999 looking for a fight, and promoters built Abbott accordingly.

Some gimmicks are just plain tacky. In the WWF, Mark Calloway was given the Undertaker gimmick with the premise that he had once worked in a funeral home. That, actually, was not true. Later in his career, Undertaker was linked by bloodlines to Kane. The WWF storytellers wrote that Kane had been burned in an accidental fire when he was a kid by none other than Undertaker—hence, Kane's mask. Not only are they not brothers, but if Glen Jacobs took off his Kane mask, fans would know the truth. Few fans, though, actually

Scars aside, Abby is just a doll

Commercially sold action figures are plenty and fans can find current stars at virtually every toy store in the country. But how many Stings, Hulk Hogans, and Goldbergs can one person have? How about a blood-stained Abdullah the Butcher doll? The folks at Figures Inc. had a bright idea and introduced a new Legends of Pro Wrestling line of figures, including Abdullah. The set also showcases Killer Kowalski, King Kong Bundy, and Ivan Putski. Naturally, collectors have the option of getting a blood-stained edition of each figure. They are all available through mail order (and even in some stores) for under $20 each. Not a bad price for a bloody Abdullah the Butcher doll. At least for the authors of this book, it's a good deal.

believed the tale. But it's part of the story and no matter how wildly conceived the story is, wrestling fans always seem ready to be entertained.

Even so, promoters strived for realness, as realism was, and always will be, part of the fascination behind great wrestling gimmicks. How real, or fake, a gimmick is can add mystique to the character. Some gimmicks were ideas spun off from movies and comic books. Chris Champion was a Ninja Turtle. The Road Warriors were born from the Mel Gibson film of the same name. Some wrestlers, for whatever reason, just didn't make it on their own; maybe they were too tall or too short, but when they are given a unique gimmick, their career blossoms. Kimala the Ugandan Giant was told years ago he had a bad heart and doctors told him he wouldn't be able to wrestle for more than five minutes at a time. But once he was given the Kimala gimmick, which called for him to demolish his opponents in quick time, he added another 10 years onto his career.

Dewy Robertson was a solid amateur wrestler before he broke into the professional ranks, but he never hooked on as a marketable talent until he painted his face green and blue, cut patches out of his hair, and called himself The Missing Link. With his new gimmick, Robertson was a main-event star in World Class and the WWF in the early 1980s. He actually continued wrestling well into his 50s, a time when wrestlers are usually long since retired.

Often the best gimmicks are simply an extension of a wrestler's real life. Steve Austin sure likes his beer and Shawn Michaels really is a ladies man. Maybe that's why their gimmicks are so successful. Gimmicks like the tough guy Stan Hansen and out-of-control Bruiser Brody were successful because their realism was in the ring. Before cable television, part of the realism came from not seeing the wrestler outside of articles in fan magazines. Pampero Firpo's wild hair and the theater of the Mummy had to be seen to be believed. Because fans from other parts of the country never saw these wrestlers live, the suspense added to their mystique.

Like bad movies, almost everyone has a

Billy Graham, middle, with Bugsy McGraw, left, and Bruiser Brody.

Dr. D, David Schultz, struts around the ring with his newly won belt.

ability in and out of the ring and make him a star just by talking for him. When John Studd and King Kong Bundy teamed up, their manager, Bobby Heenan, made them sound like they could end the world if they got angry. Managers also helped a wrestler's gimmick by making it seem that his protégé would be the man to dethrone the baby-faced champion. Jimmy Hart had a whole stable of freaks and monsters in Memphis to take down Jerry "The King" Lawler in the early 1980s. Wrestlers with oddball gimmicks were always top challengers for the champion's belt.

Some gimmicks are so ridiculous, all we can do as fans is laugh. In South America, genius promoters sold a "wrestler" named The Invisible Man. His opponent certainly seemed dim. All a wrestler did when taking on the Invisible Man was move around the ring like he was getting beat up by a phantom wrestler. The Ding Dongs were actually an idea in WCW as a take-off on the fun-loving Bushwackers in the WWF. When the Ding Dongs hit the ring, the bells that were attached to their outfits would fall off when

King Kong Bundy.

guilty pleasure for poorly planned gimmicks. Outback Jack and Red Rooster added laughs to WWF programming. Today's gimmicks are more sophisticated, with the use of technical glitz and pyrotechnics such as Oz, Glacier, and Kane. Kevin Sullivan was a master at wild characters that were too bad not to like. Sullivan created "Purple Haze" Mark Lewin in Florida and a bevy of strange beings in WCW (Evad Sullivan, the Shark, the Zodiac). Many times, there is no reason why we should enjoy these characters, but we do. Isaac Yankem was no Ric Flair and Bastion Booger was no Rey Mysterio Jr. But for some reason, they were just as entertaining as their technical counterparts.

Having a manager sometimes meant whether or not a gimmick was successful. Managers could take a wrestler with little they hit the mat. Thankfully for fans, that gimmick did not last long.

Sometimes, just one little part of a wrestler's personality gives them a marketable gimmick. Sometimes, it was the little things that made the most impact. "Crazy" Luke Graham and Rick Steiner used to bark at themselves. Wild Bull Curry looked like a maniac with his wild eyebrows and caused riots wherever he went.

Wrestling's first gimmick wrestler

Maurice Tillet brought fame to Sweden in the 1940s and 1950s as the French Angel. He had a handicap few can overcome—Acromegaly—a disease that Jack Merrick, the Elephant Man, suffered from. In America, Tillet became a heroic ring star. When promoters glanced at Tillet, they saw potential at the box office, but U.S. fans refused to jeer a real-life human oddity and as a result, Tillet had a very successful ring career. Leave it to promoters to capitalize on a good thing. With Tillet's success, promoters used the "Angel" character often. After Tillet, Polish Angel, Swedish Angel, Czech Angel, Irish Angel, Golden Angel, Canadian Angel, and even Lady Angel followed. With as may as ten incarnations of the gimmick, "Swedish Angel" Tor Johnson added the word Super to his name. Johnson was a main event performer in the 1940s and 1950s and parlayed

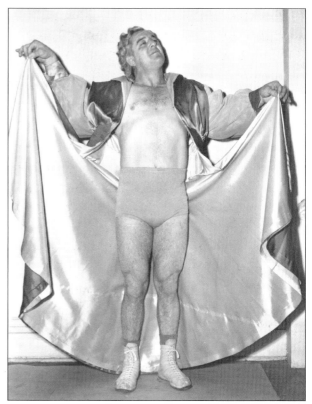
Gorgeous George.

his ring talents into Hollywood film roles. Johnson was a classic movie villain who hung out with the likes of Ronald Regan, but he also had a unique sense of humor and appeared in Ed Wood's "B" flicks with star Bela Lugosi.

The 6-foot-5 barrel-chested Ox Baker is one of the only villains who battled into the future. The bald menace, who was known for his thick mustache and heart-punch maneuver, reached the future in a Death match against "Snake Plisken" (Kurt Russell) in the

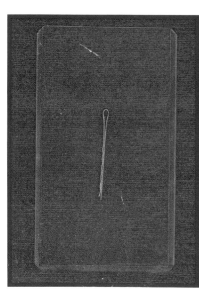

— Wrestling pins aren't only on the mat —

Gorgeous George was quite a character and there is no denying the 1950s star lived his gimmick. His collection is currently managed by the staff at Slammer's Gym in Studio City, Calif. One of the real treasures of his collection is the famous "Georgie Pins." These bobby pins, made in 24- and 14k gold, were worn by George. The wrestler was also known to give the pins as gifts to his female fans. Before George bestowed a pin on a fan, however, he made the recipient recite this loyal oath: "I do solemnly swear and promise to never confuse this gold Georgie Pin with a common, ordinary bobby pin, so help me, Gorgeous George." Items such as the Georgie Pins, atomizers, candelabra, and robes are highly valuable pieces of memorabilia.

1981 movie "Escape from New York." Although Baker won't be remembered as a tactical wizard in the ring, his ugly mug kept him a touring main-event star from 1950 to 1980.

Blonde locks were his ticket to fame

One of the greatest gimmicks ever was the one played by the legendary Gorgeous George. George Wagner was a tough guy to be sure. Born in Seward, Nebraska, he worked as a laborer by day and wrestled by night. He just couldn't earn a living at either profession until he made a complete make-over and became the "Human Orchid" Gorgeous George. As Gorgeous George, he dyed his hair platinum blonde, donned a purple silk cape, and was ushered into the ring with his wife, Betty. Wagner became the man fans loved to hate and in doing so, he became one the top-drawing attractions of the 1940s. He was wrestling's first "must see" performer.

George later added a hairdresser to accompany him to the ring who would roll out a red carpet and spray the ring with a disinfectant before the match started. On is way to the ring, he would give lady spectators gold-plated bobby pins or roses. Wagner was the first wrestler to play into homophobic taunts and the ruse worked. His outrageousness spawned wrestling's era of extravagance. Muhammed Ali once said it was after seeing Gorgeous George that he decided to become an outrageous boxer. In 1949, Wagner reached the pinnacle of wrestling stardom by headlining at Madison Square Garden against Ernie Dusk. Wagner also legally changed his name to Gorgeous George. For 20 strong years, few wrestlers filled the seats like Wagner. To this day, performers who push the envelope owe a nod or a wink to the one and only "Human Orchid."

The Grand Wizard and Ox Baker.

Gimmick matches, promotions are the roots of wrestling

Gimmick matches are nothing new. Whether it is Battle Royal, Bunkhouse, Texas Death, Cage, or Brass Knuckles matches, wrestling has always been filled with a large number of gimmick matches. Recently, nontraditional matches have become a widely used technique to attract fans.

Two years ago, "hardcore" became a household word in pro wrestling. The WWF put a hardcore title on Mankind (Mick Foley) in a move that seemed temporary at best. Foley's matches with all comers often took place in the strangest of place: dumpsters, boiler rooms, lavatories, on car rooftops, parking lots, and locker rooms. His matches were unbelievably entertaining, as the wrestlers usually enhanced the new settings by using blunt objects to hit each other with.

Not only were fisticuffs and head butts allowed in these hardcore matches, but also allowed were fire extinguishers, plungers, stop signs, garbage cans, and other assorted garage-sale leftovers. To the masses, the matches were unique and caught on with the fans and a new division was born.

Since then, the WWF's hardcore division, followed by WCW's own hardcore division, has become a staple on television and their influence has trickled to promotions all over the country.

Mankind may have brought them to a national phenomenon, but hardcore matches were hardly original.

Seemingly, the idea—in some form or another—has been passed down from generations previous. In the United States, ECW made hardcore matches a way of life. Since the group's inception, wrestlers using garbage-can lids in bouts has been almost mandatory. When the late Eddie Gilbert, who was known as a matchmaking mastermind, first helped pre-ECW promotions in the early 1990s, he picked up on a style that was being used to even more violent extremes in Japan's Frontier Martial Arts group. Gilbert, it is believed, brought that idea to the U.S. and Paul Dangerously had since cultivated the idea. Dangerously used wrestlers like Mick Foley, Terry Funk, Tommy Dreamer, Sabu, and the Public Enemy who were willing to scar their bodies in hardcore bouts.

When ECW was hitting a stride with hardcore matches in the late 1990s, the WWF

Gary Hart and Abdullah the Butcher.

used the idea to juice up its own shows—that's when Mankind became the Federation's first hardcore champ. And the rest is history.

Long-time fans will take issue with ECW having created "hardcore" in the U.S. The Original Sheik was hardcore in the 1970s. In Mississippi, a now-famous match between Jerry Lawler and Bill Dundee against the Moodogs (a team that oddly enough featured Wayne Ferris, a.k.a the Honkytonk

Man) spilled over into a nearby concessions stand, where the wrestlers used jars of mustard, mops, and popcorn containers as foreign objects.

When and where were hardcore matches really born? The answer probably lies in this question: How has the hardcore mentality matured and evolved over the years?

No one will dispute that today's hardcore matches are much different than those in the 1970s. Back then, something as simple as a folding chair would get fans' interests peaked. Now, hardcore has become an industry all to itself, as modern-day warriors use anything imaginable to make a match unforgettable.

For much of the 1990s, FMW was the king of extreme promotions. In 1990, Atsushi Onita's group became a popular Japanese alternative. Using everything from barbed wire to exploding cage matches, Onita became a Hall of Fame candidate through his essays in violence. He was hospitalized numerous times and has received so many stitches for his wounds, he would probably be the Guinness Book's uncrowned stitch king. The promotion's "death matches" became the talk of wrestling and for a time, FMW's wrestlers lost more blood than anyone. Mick Foley, then known as Cactus Jack, traveled to FMW for almost three years and partook in some of the group's most brutal matches. Funk, Tarzan Goto, Ricky Fuji, Mike Awesome, Sheik, Sabu, and Horace Boulder were constants and became instant legends for their daringness to be involved.

Today, groups like Xtreme Pro Wrestling and Combat Zone have taken wrestling into the deepest caverns of violence. The groups regularly feature barbed wire, broken glass, fire, and thumbtacks as common weapons used in the ring.

The wilder the better

Promoters will try anything, from the unique and entertaining, to the absurd. The latter was accomplished in the WWF when Rick Martel took on Jake Roberts in a blindfold match, the first noted attempt of this type. Both Roberts and Martel wore blindfolds—fans insist the fabric was seethough—and the two stammered around the ring for 10 minutes. Roberts, by the way, liked to bring a snake with him to the ring. Another match involving animals was the WWF's hell-in-a-kennel bout between Al Snow and Big Bossman. The two wrestlers were locked inside a regular cage. Then, dogs were locked inside a barrier outside the first cage. In theory, the dogs would "attack" the wrestlers if they got out of their cage. The result was both horrible and laughable. The wrestlers did their part to make the match tolerable, but the dogs just stood and barked at each other. Promoters haven't tried this match again. During the 1950s, wrestling bears were a popular attraction and women wrestlers Alma Mills, Lulu LeMar, and Mae Young were all known for taking on the animals.

One crazy match that reached wide appeal in the 1980s was the scaffold match. Bill Dundee, a 5-9 former trapeze artist in

The Bruiser.

Jimmy Valiant.

nacle in 1986 when the Jim Cornette-led Midnight Express fought the Road Warriors at Starrcade. Dennis Condrey, Bobby Eaton, and Cornette all took the two-foot-plunge from atop the scaffold. Cornette injured his knee badly as a result.

In Puerto Rico, fire was used for the first time in the mid-1980s; for much of the 1970s, Puerto Rico was known as an island of blood. Carlos Colon, Bruiser Brody, and Abdullah the Butcher were the forefathers of out-of-the-ring brawling. To culminate his feud with Hercules Ayala, Colon promoted a ring-of-fire match, where the ring ropes were doused with flammable liquid and lit on fire. Colon tried to burn Ayala, while attending fans sat in awe. While it is a dangerous bout for obvious reasons, the wrestlers are careful not to burn each other on accident. In later years, fire became increasingly accepted as a regular match. The 20,000 fans that attended the Colon-Ayala match made promoters realize that no matter the danger, craziness is best.

Australia, knew it would take more than normal matches to get his character accepted, so he met Jerry Lawler in a scaffold bout. High above the ring was a scaffold that stretched across the whole ring. The object of the match was that a wrestler only would win by throwing his opponent off the scaffolding. The scaffold match reached its pin-

Projecting fear is what builds the mystique behind gimmick matches. Timing and letting the fans see every movement of the wrestlers portrays the feeling of danger. It's similar to a maestro with a wand.

Cage matches have offered fans some of the most memorable, and forgettable, bouts.

All of Mankind fell for this guy

Mick Foley had no idea when he wrote nearly 700 handwritten pages for his national-al best-selling book, Tales of Blood and Sweatsocks, that the book's success would make him a cross-over star. The movie "Beyond the Mat" didn't hurt, either. As Mankind, Foley also became a pitchman for Chef Boyardee. The ads on television were a laugh and Foley loved every minute of it. Given away as promotional items, these life-size cardboard cut-outs are a special find for collectors. For about $40, the stand-ups are being sold through the Internet. Just think, for minimal bucks, you, too, can have a hardcore icon right in your home.

Haystacks Calhoun tosses J.C. Dykes back into the ring after he tries to escape.

Seeing Jimmy Snuka leap from atop a cage in his feud with Bob Backlund made such an impression on a young Mick Foley that the future Cactus Jack wanted to become a wrestler the moment he saw Snuka's leap. When there is a cage match, fans can almost assure themselves that they will see blood—and when they don't, it can be a disappointment. The NWA promoted caged War-Games matches and the idea was solid: two rings surrounded by one giant cage. Unfortunately, the cage took more than 40 minutes to assemble and often those matches were short and bloodless.

There have been many gimmick matches which were often used to settle a feud. Indian-strap matches gave Wahoo McDaniel and Jay Strongbow sustained main-event status. Billy White Wolf may have engaged in the first Indian death match, however. In 1962, during a feud with Tony Borne, the two settled the grudge in the death bout. The two were tied together with a 10-foot strap and to win, a man had to drag his foe to all four corners of the ring, and, of course, the strap

was used as a weapon.

The late Boris Malenko was the father of Russian chain matches, an event similar to a death match. Dusty Rhodes was the so-called king of the bull-rope match. "Hacksaw" Jim Duggan once battled Ted DiBiase in a tuxedo match. Coal Miner's Glove matches and brass-knuckles matches were also used in the 1980s.

The NWA territory featured the bunkhouse-stampede match, which was an "anything goes" battle royal. Other variations, like the lumberjack matches, would see wrestlers line up around ringside and stomp fellow wrestlers who fell out of the ring. Battle royals were big in the 1960s, but are mere afterthoughts today. Often times, the match would determine the No. 1 contender for the championship. Promoters would dub battle royals the most dangerous of any match, but many wrestlers saw the attraction as a night off because it didn't require them to work very hard.

Of late, table and ladder matches have been a hit. The Dudley Boyz brought the table gimmick to the WWF with them from ECW. Throwing an opponent through a folding table is the only way to win this spectacle. In ladder bouts, a metal ladder is used as a weapon. Edge, Christian, and the Hardy Boys have been highly innovative with the maneuvers they have dreamed of in ladder matches. The high standard for ladder matches was set in the Shawn Michaels-Razor Ramon match from Wrestlemania.

Sky Low Low drop kicks Joey Russell during a midget tag-team match.

Tiger Jeet Singh, Kurt Von Hess, and Mr. Hito, from left, work out in Japan.

Cactus Jack (Mick Foley) and Ox Baker.

New Jack, left, Tommy Dreamer (atop ladder) and Spike Dudley celebrate after a ladder match.

He was huge in a big man's world

William Calhoun was just a good old boy at heart. Born in 1934 in Texas, he got into wrestling in his early 20s. It was a natural sport for Calhoun. His size, which was a legitimate 601 pounds, made him a prime attraction for professional wrestling. During his career, he was known as Haystacks Calhoun and wrestled all over the world, but the Eastern U.S. turned into a home for the large Texan. He regularly wrestled in New York—as witnessed by this 1964 Island Gardens program—and was a popular attraction for many promoters. In 1957, Calhoun took part in the heaviest match ever against the 720-pound Happy Humphrey in Georgia. Fans of the 1950s and 1960s remember vividly the size that Calhoun carried with him—and that size alone makes him a true legend of wrestling.

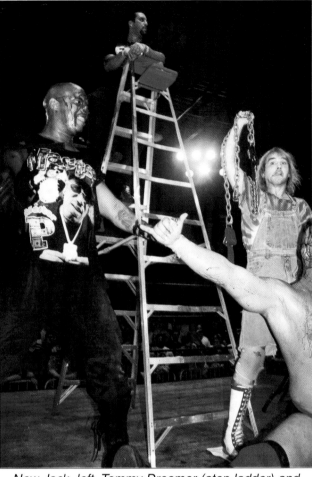

ISLAND GARDEN

PROGRAM

HAYSTACKS CALHOUN

FRIDAY, NOVEMBER 6 1964   Price 25¢

The Mummy.

Tiger Jeet Singh.

Abdullah the Butcher vs. Thunderbolt Patterson.

With a crazy look in his eyes, Terry Funk wields a
flaming branding iron.

Sabu sets up a table for an unsuspecting foe.

Rikki Starr was wrestling's only trained ballet star.

Little Bruiser.

Public Enemy made their careers by
taking garbage cans to the extreme.

The notorious "Mr. Q," Quasimodo from England.

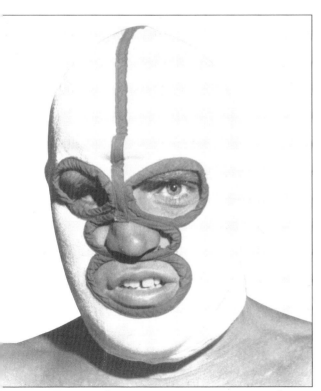

The Intelligent Sensational Destroyer, a one-time
world heavyweight champion.

Sabu and Terry Funk in a chain match.

Bad News Allen Coage in a Judo-jacket match with George Wells.

Lord Littlebrook.

The Convict (a.k.a. Uncle Elmer).

Mongol and King Curtis.

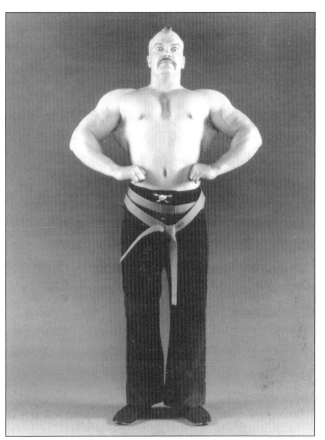

Tijo Khan.

Perry Saturn gets ready to throw a chair.

Jesse "The Body" Ventura pumps some iron, and strikes a muscleman pose.

Chapter 11

Totally Tag Teams

Whether it's look-a-like wrestlers, brothers, or ex-rivals siding together for the sake of goodness, tag-team wrestling employs an important aspect to any wrestling show. One of the first tag-team matches was held in Houston in 1936 that included Whiskers Savage and Milo Steinborn against Fazul Mohammed and Tiger Daula. The first tag-team matches were said to be all four men in the ring at one time. Soon promoters felt more comfortable with the idea of one-on-one action in the ring and having to tag your partner to bring him in the ring.

The best tag teams have a certain chemistry that mixes perfectly. In the recording industry, Glen Frye and Don Henley teamed and were a magical presence as the rock band, The Eagles. Wrestling is no different. The perfect teams have a history of being two men that have talents which accentuate the others.

Since the early days, tag teams have evolved considerably. Over time, partnerships were based on common bonds, like brotherhood, father-and-son, and even ring attire. Some of the first tag teams to wear identical ring outfits were Red and Lou Bastien and the Fabulous Kangaroos. Certainly, having the two dress alike made them more marketable and gave the wrestlers careers longevity as draws at the arenas.

Brothers and look-a-likes

Brother combinations have usually been successful. Although few teams were actually blood relatives, the gimmicks these teams used fit perfectly in tag-team competition. Brother teams that did well were Gilberts, the Funks, the Guererros, the Toloses, the Youngbloods, the Steiners, Randy Savage, and Lanny Poffo just to name a few. And though brother acts were generally considered to be hero types, at some point, they all turned heel eventually. Chris, Tom, and

The Fabulous Freebirds.

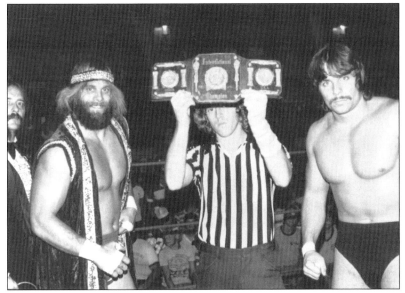

Randy "Macho Man" Savage, left, and his brother, Leaping Lanny Poffo, before their title match.

them like they were part of a family. Today, that same feeling is bestowed on Too Cool in the WWF.

There is a simple reason for the advent of tag-team wrestling. To promoters, it mixes things up on a card and creates more interest and also gives promoters more material to work with. As the years have passed, tag teams have stayed for other reasons. Often a tag team will combine two wrestlers who, when wrestling alone, are without charisma. Another purpose was to join two wrestlers who brought different talents to the table. Sometimes, a wrestler who didn't have a gift for gab would be joined with someone who could do great interviews. Jesse Ventura was a wild man on the microphone, but was a limited wrestler. When he joined with the technically superior Adrian Adonis, promoters struck gold. Ricky Morton was a great talker who was the spokesman for himself and Robert Gibson as the Rock & Roll Express. Separately, the two would have had short careers—but together, they offered much more.

Some tag teams are born out of necessity. Wrestling thrives on big, powerful men, but sometimes wrestlers who are small find suc-

George Zaharias were one of the first famed brother tandems. Some like the Funks (Dory Jr. and Terry) and the Briscos were real blood brothers, while others, like the Road Warriors and the Valiant Brothers, were simply partners in war.

It seems the brothers who were not actually related were relegated to be heels. The Valiants (Johnny, Jimmy, and Jerry), the Fargos (Jackie and Don), Beverly Brothers (Blake and Beau), the Kalmikoffs (Karol and Ivan), the Strongbows (Jules and Jay), the Andersons (Gene, Ole and Arn), Grahams (Crazy Luke, Dr. Jerry, Eddie, and Superstar), and Kane and the Undertaker never shared family picnics together to be sure. But the idea of their relationships was what worked to attract fans. The idea that each member would look out for his partner—at any cost—caused fans to go crazy at their dastardly deeds.

Then there were the look-a-like tandems that did well at the box office. The Masked Interns, the Superstars, the Yukon Lumberjacks, the British Bulldogs, the Hart Foundation, the Rock & Roll Express, the Midnight Rockers, Bad Company, the Assassins, the Southern Boys, and Demolition all projected the feeling they were together for a reason. Promoters pushed

Dory and Terry Funk.

cess as part of a team. Marty Janetty and Shawn Michaels toiled in the land of giants. Together, as the Midnight Rockers (and later, just the "Rockers" in the WWF), they became one of the most popular teams of the 1990s. Others who grew from that mold were the Fabulous Ones (Stan Lane and Steve Keirn), the Simpson Brothers, and the Fantastics (Bobby Fulton and Tommy Rogers).

In recent years, tag-team wrestling has evolved even further with the advent of wrestling stables. The original Four Horsemen (Ric Flair, Ole Anderson, Arn Anderson, and Tully Blanchard) and the Freebirds (Michael Hayes, Terry Gordy, and Buddy Roberts) were perhaps the first conglomerates seen in wrestling. The idea behind these teams was that any member could fight on any night. Usually, these teams were the main heel focal point of a show. Others were born out of the Four-Horseman mold. Just look around. The Radicals (Chris Benoit, Eddie Guerrero, Perry Saturn, and Dean Malenko), Degeneration X (Triple H, X-Pac, Road Dogg, and Billy Gunn), the Disciples of Apocalypse, the New World Order and others have all seen moderate to great success when joined as a unit.

In the 1960s and 1970s, it was popular to bring a special partner into a territory to team with a promotion's regular performer. Andre the Giant, Verne Gagne, Ernie Ladd, and Bill Watts were often brought in to be

The famous Vachons: Butcher and Mad Dog, world tag-team champions.

special one-time partners to fight off the established heels. Teams with connections to different parts of the world have been marketable. The Sheepherders were billed from New Zealand, the Orient Express were billed from Japan, and Elix Skipper and Lance Storm are said to be from Canada—anything to create interest.

They boogie-woogied until the dawn

From 1984 to 1986, there was arguably no better tag team than Ricky Morton and Robert Gibson, the Rock & Roll Express. Jerry Lawler has said that he first had the idea for the team while flipping through a magazine for teen-agers and thought a tag team should be created which would embrace a rock-'n'-roll theme. Wearing bandannas and coming to the ring to hard-thumping music, Morton and Gibson were reborn with their new gimmick. For young female fans especially, the Express could do no wrong. They stopped off in Mid-South and drew huge crowds before they eventually headed to Jim Crockett Promotions and the NWA/Mid-Atlantic area. With a huge fan following, the Express started a fan club under Crockett. This copy of the Rock & Roll Express magazine was mailed to fan-club members. The magazine chronicles the life of Gibson and Morton and issues can be found today from $15 to $20.

The Fabulous Kangaroos: Roy Heffernan,
Red Berry, and Al Costello.

An autograph is a sign of a real collectible

Autographs are a natural collectible in wrestling and it seems like every fan has a story to tell about the day they got their favorite performer to sign a piece of paper. This autograph book from the 1960s, worth about $10 today, was sold by a local promoter for fans to have signed as the wrestlers went home after the card. There are many sellers of autographs of the current stars and often they are written on color-promotion photos. Some of the more popular are the Undertaker and the Rock. Each are worth from $40 to $50. Old-time wrestlers are also in demand. A few of the most valuable autographs are of Jim Londos ($120) and Stanislaus Zbyszko ($100).

World tag-team champs Jesse Ventura and Adrian Adonis "The East-West Connection."

Andre the Giant and Chief Strongbow.

Bruno Sammartino and Dom DeNucci.

The Terminators introduce themselves to correspondent Marvin Joel Rubin.

Japan tag-teamers Mr. Saito and Mr. Fuji.

Larry Hennig and Harley Race.

One of the great global and WWWF tag teams: Miguel Perez and Argentina Rocca.

Blackjack Mulligan and Jack Lanza.

Sheepherders.

Ripping off the Caped Crusader

There are a few reasons why wrestlers wear masks. Through history, they often did actually want to hide their identity. Having a mask also meant the promoter could use them twice on a card—once with the mask, once without—and get a bigger paycheck that night. Sometimes, a wrestler wore a mask to protect his identity for a future run as headliner. Whatever the reason, none was a more commercial and blatant take-off than Tony Marino's Batman character from the 1960s. This October 1966 issue of Wrestling Revue has Marino and an unknown sidekick (named Robin, of course) featured on the cover. Marino mainly used the gimmick on the East Coast. He did not wrestle long with the gimmick, but it stands as one of the more comical personas in wrestling history. The issue can be bought for under $20.

Lou Albano and The Valiants.

Scott Hall and Curt Hennig,
AWA world tag-team champions.

The Interns.

Dino Bravo and Greg Gagne.

Booker T and Stevie Ray are "Harlem Heat."

Rick and Scott Steiner.

Rick "The Rock" ` Morton and Robert Gibson, Rock & Roll Express.

Jim Cornette, center, and his Midnight Express.

Chapter 12

Getting a Hold on Their Opponent

Like anything in professional wrestling, the holds and maneuvers used in a match have changed greatly over the years. But, as some forms of today's wrestling by-products show, even those changes have come full circle.

In the early 20th Century, shoot-style wrestling ruled. Shooting, or hooking, as it was sometimes called, referred to legitimate moves born out of submission moves from the martial arts genres. Shoot wrestling is far different than what a fan may see in a Hardy Boys versus Dudley Boys match in the World Wrestling Federation. The style is more of a slow, plotting, yet painful, combination of moves. It is more inclined to look like an amateur wrestling bout than what the public would consider professional wrestling.

The moves used in this style were leg locks, ankle locks, and arm-bars that saw both contestants on the mat, rather than today's vertical style. The 1908 three-hour bout between Frank Gotch and George Hackenschmidt, for example, was a match very indicative of the day. Most of the match took place on the mat, as each man tried to wear down his opponent in a true test of wills. While ropes were used around the ring, wrestling at this point had not taken the turn to using them to perform moves.

Wrestling remained in that style well into the 1920s, but as the sport grew out of legitimacy into a rehearsed show, the idea of actual-

ly hurting an opponent largely subsided. Even so, from the 1920s to 1930s, wrestlers, in an effort to keep the mystique alive that wrestling was real, most still used versions of the moves born out of shooting. Only now, there were different variations. The headlock and figure-four leg lock, moves still used today, grew in popularity. By the 1930s, moves were conjured up to fit a particular wrestler's personality. Jim Londos, a noted scientific wrestler, made his trademark move a basic arm lock. Strangler Lewis used to intimidate the audience into thinking his

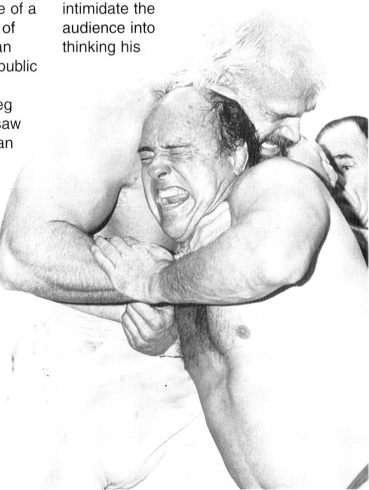

Jesse Ventura puts the choke on Verne Gagne.

headlock was so powerful, he could literally squeeze a man to his death. Of course, that was just part of the show.

As promoters clued into the show aspect of pro wrestling, maneuvers changed with the times. Gus Sonnenberg used the flying tackle, which connected him to his college football days at Dartmouth University, where he wrestled in the 1930s. Antonino Rocca was probably the first wrestler to utilize high-flying moves in his arsenal. Rocca, an East-Coast star, regularly performed drop kicks and basic moves off the ropes. There was implied danger when a wrestler climbed to the top of the ropes and crashed down in his opponents. Some commissions in different areas of the county even outlawed such moves, not knowing that wrestling was in fact scripted.

From the 1950s to present, wrestling holds and moves evolved significantly. As one wrestler seemingly took a risk by performing more death-defying feats, another was right behind him with an even more amazing move. After awhile, outdoing a fellow per-former was a way to become known and marketable in the eyes of promoters.

Today, few can argue that professional wrestlers are pure entertainers with an eye for the dramatic. While the character that a wrestler portrays accounts for much of that, the maneuvers that he or she uses do just as much to create the character as interview style or costume. Now, the finishing move

The Spoiler prepares to deliver a leg drop on Steve Williams.

that a wrestler uses is a big part of their identity. The reason for that is simple: Largely, a finishing move (the move that is

Are you ready for a wrestling movie?

Everyone laughed—some even fell over—when David Arquette became World Championship Wrestling champion. Previously known as the AT&T phone guy, Arquette parlayed his goofiness into a role in the fea-ture film "Ready to Rumble." The movie featured WCW characters like Diamond Dallas Page, Bam Bam Bigelow, and Saturn. Movie posters, like this one, can be found for $20. Arquette, though, had the last laugh. After the movie was released, scriptwriters thought it would be interest-ing to let Arquette win the championship on WCW television. The reign lasted only one week, but fans won't soon forget when a wacky Hollywood actor held the prestigious WCW title.

Chris Taylor's mighty Olympic plex.

Tito Santana drop kicks John Studd.

used to put away an opponent before a pin fall) is used exclusively by that wrestler. Steve Austin has the "Stone Cold Stunner," Scott Steiner uses the "Steiner Recliner," and Rob Van Dam uses the "Van Terminator."

Finishing moves are one of the most recognizable aspects to a wrestler's personality. Hulk Hogan is synonymous with the leg drop. For much of the 1980s, crowds would cheer and get on their feet when one of Hogan's foes was the victim of that move. It was, and still is, rare, when an opponent actually gets up after a finishing move is applied or performed.

Some wrestlers have taken great pride in new innovations in moves. Many of today's high-flying moves, like a huricanrana and moonsault, were born in Japan and Mexico.

Greg Valentine's explosive elbow smash.

Jimmy Snuka about to put a flying body press on Mike Sharpe.

Often, an American wrestler will watch videos of matches overseas and try to imitate the move in the United States. In the late 1980s, when Keiji Muto came to the United States for the first time as the Great Muta, he brought with him the moonsault. The move is performed by standing on the top turnbuckle and flipping backward onto an opponent. It was the first time anyone in America had seen the move and as a result, fans were electrified. That one move seemingly caused a revolution in professional wrestling. The moonsault is now part of a wrestler's regular arsenal. Even at age 40, Terry Funk was performing moonsaults with the best of them.

Today's wrestling often looks more like a high-wire act than a wrestling match. The Hardy Boys, Rey Mysterio, Juventud Guererra, and Sabu have been genuine innovators by employing the most spectacular moves fans have ever seen in the USA. These wrestlers are certainly not afraid of injury. Their arsenals consist mainly of moves in the air, full of twists and turns and crashing through tables and chairs.

But some of wrestling's old days remain. Kurt Angle is not opposed to using an ankle lock, a move symbolic of his amateur wrestling career. Ric Flair used the figure four up to his semi-retirement in 2000. Even Austin uses the simple Lou Thesz press as an homage to the former NWA champion.

In Japan, and even here in the U.S. to an extent, submission moves made famous by Gotch and others in the early 1900s are

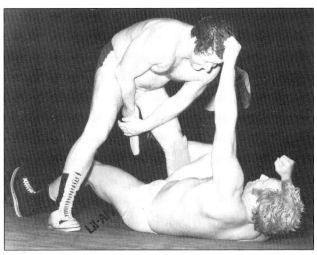

Terry Funk applies a spinning toehold on Nick Bockwinkel.

Jack Brisco with a leglock on Giant Baba. Brisco and Giant Baba met several times in Japan, but Brisco was able to narrowly retain the title each time.

He can't act, but he sure can wrestle

The Vince McMahon marketing machine was chugging at a nice clip in 1989, when Hulk Hogan starred in his first full-length feature film, "No Holds Barred." Not surprisingly, the plot of the movie concerned Hogan's ascendance to the top of a wrestling group to meet a hated villain (played by Tiny Lister) in the face of an evil promoter (i.e. McMahon). The WWF managed to turn the movie plot into a wrestling storyline that culminated in a Summerslam main event. Wrestlers, like Roddy Piper and Jesse Ventura, have taken part in movies for many years. "No Holds Barred" movie posters and advertising are unique collectibles. They hold with them a part of wrestling that has made the silver screen. Full color posters are available for less than $60.

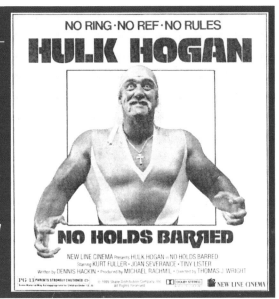

gaining in popularity. Promotions like Pride and Rings, which are pro-wrestling off-shoots, and the Ultimate Fighting Championships, highlight bouts with submission and shoot-wrestling moves. In Japan, these promotions are generally legitimate and have become immensely popular.

Nearly 100 years after Gotch held the world's wrestling championship, performers of today would make him proud to know his style did not die with the times.

Dick Shikat shows how to apply a textbook arm bar.

Al Snow in an elbow lock.

Billy Robinson forces Josef Zaranoff to submit to an arm bar.

Edwardo Carpentier goes acrobatic on John Vander.

Stan Hansen and Paul Orndorff do battle.

Nikolai Volkoff applies his nerve grip to Dusty Rhodes.

Bill Watts performs the "bulldog" throw from the '60s.

Johnny Valentine gives Eddie Graham a forearm smash.

Getting a Hold on Their Opponent

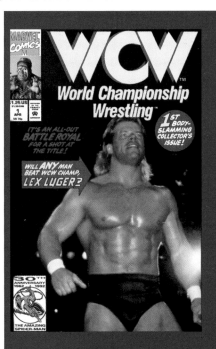

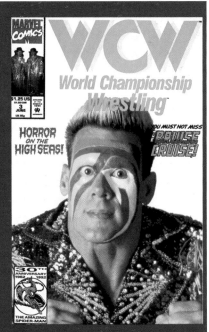

Who knew P.N. News was a collectible?

Marvel Comics tried its hand at wrestling comic books in 1992 with a special World Championship Wrestling special set. The handful of issues that was released was not overly popular, but the comics were well done. The first three covers, shown here, feature Lex Luger, Sting, and Ron Simmons. Inside, fans thought it was unique to find the likes of Z-Man, Flyin' Brian, P.N. News, and Arn Anderson in comic form. Now, each issue will fetch up to $10. Marvel stopped selling the line shortly after it began and has not returned to wrestling since.

Tiger Mask drop kicks Black Tiger.

Dr. Death about to press slam Rick Steiner.

Sting applies an arm lock on Animal of the Road Warriors.

Abdullah the Butcher drops his big elbow on Giant Baba during a match in Japan.

Chapter 13

Connecting the Dots

"Professional wrestling is the theater of the absurd." – *Sports Illustrated*, 1954.

Wrestling, in all its glory, pomp, and circumstance is arguably the greatest show on earth. No performers work harder at pleasing the crowd, their peers, and themselves. Whether it's in front of 50 people in Every City USA or 50,000 at the Tokyo Dome, wrestling is spellbinding, thrilling, dramatic, engaging, at times humorous, and also violent. On any given night, hundreds, if not thousands, will put their hearts and souls into the wrestling ring. And for good rea-

son—at least to the wrestlers, anyway.

From the 1960s to the 1980s, wrestling territories had to exist. The product promoters offered was simply too good to allow just one champion to appear in one city each night, as had happened during the first half of the 20th Century. Promoters, in most major cities, jumped at the opportunity to hold live wrestling in their cities, from Portland to San Francisco to St. Louis to Atlanta and Pittsburgh. The times were good and several hundred wrestlers stayed active.

With the advent of cable television in the 1980s, fans had no choice but to turn on the

Early champion wrestlers like Harley Race gave way to champs like Kevin Nash.

tube. Georgia Championship Wrestling on WTBS was the first to explode. Dusty Rhodes, Ric Flair, Tommy Rich, the Freebirds, the Junkyard Dog, Buzz Sawyer, Harley Race, and dozens more seemed to jump off the magazine pages into our lives. The World Wrestling Federation, and others, soon followed. Prior to cable, only fans in the East Coast were privileged to see the WWF's stars. Whether it was guilty-pleasure favorites like S.D. Jones and Salvatore Bellomo or true champions like Bob Backlund and Bruno Sammartino, wrestling fans were given their first opportunity to see the stars on a national scale. Even smaller promotions had chances on cable. California Championship Wrestling and Texas All-Star were seen weekly. Japanese women were performing death-defying feats on, of all channels, the defunct Financial News Network. Wrestling from Hawaii and Bill Watts' UWF had loyal followings.

Then, in a flash, wrestling as we knew it was gone.

The explosion of the 1980s gave WWF owner Vince McMahon reason to puff his chest. Wrestling was seen on USA, MTV and NBC television networks, Wrestlemania was a pay-per-view success, and the WWF ran as many as three live shows per night. The

Chris Benoit utilizes submissions regularly, just as Frank Gotch, Wayne Munn, and Farmer Burns did back in their day.

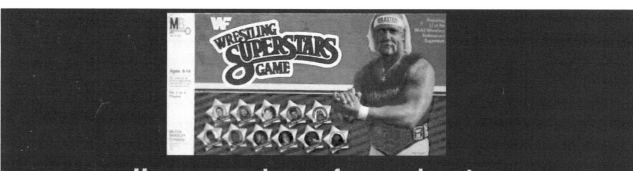

Hogan game leaves fans seeing stars

Hulk Hogan was the king of 1980s wrestling. When he surfaced in the World Wrestling Federation in 1984, he was tailor-made to be the crossover star that the WWF wanted to put on the map. Hogan's role extended well beyond championships and headline matches, though. Through careful marketing and promotion, Hogan became a brand name. Licensees joined the WWF in droves and hundreds of products were sold with his likeness. This Milton Bradley WWF Superstars board game was one. All of the major names of the day were part of the game including Randy Savage, Andre the Giant, and Jake Roberts. Current fans are always looking for mid-1980s memorabilia. In good to excellent condition, this game—not Triple H—can be found for $40.

Rob Van Dam, left, and The Rock have followed in the footsteps of Woody Strode and Tor Johnson and have moved from the ring to the big screen.

WWF was everywhere. By the 1990s, fans grew tired of the WWF and wrestling in general. Whether fans were bored of Hulk Hogan or the accusations of McMahon hiding a steroid-abuse problem in his company played a bigger toll than originally thought, the WWF saw lean years early in the decade. By the end of the decade, though, Steve Austin had picked up where Hogan left off and opened the door for Triple H and the Rock to join in an even bigger boom.

Full Circle Still

The old adage that wrestling never really changes was never more true by the late 1990s. Pay-per-views clearly had replaced regularly run territorial shows like in the 1970s. Territories would build toward weekly or monthly live shows. Now, the major wrestling companies built toward their cable TV specials.

Once again, we see wrestlers everywhere. Austin is on network programming, the Rock and Dallas Page are in movies, and even New Jack and Rob Van Dam are on film. The new-age wrestlers were simply carrying on the tradition laid by their forefathers. Gorgeous George, "Hard Boiled" Haggerty, Lenny Montana, Woody Strode, Tor Johnson, Terry Funk, and countless others appeared on film and TV long before Austin and Van Dam ever did. It only seems that in a world of the Internet and satellite television, today's wrestlers are a whole lot bigger than life.

Has wrestling really changed all that much? Hardly. It may have been modernized and it certainly has become a faster-paced event, but what we see now has always been around.

Critics call today's wrestling demeaning to women. Didn't Gorgeous George demean his valets? Was not the Fabulous Moolah once known as the "Slave Girl?" And what about drivel like the FOX network's show, "Temptation Island?" As promoter Bruce Hart once prophesied, "Wrestling only mirrors society."

From steel cages to ladders, wrestling has utilized gimmick matches throughout its history. At top, left, George "The Animal" Steele looks a bit wary of entering the steel cage, most likely because an enraged Bruno Sammartino was waiting for him. At right are Kevin Sullivan and Dusty Rhodes in a classic chain match. At bottom left, Roddy Piper is ready to rope an opponent in a bull-rope match; at right is a bloodied New Jack after a ladder match.

Wrestling continually digs into its 100-year-old bag of tricks. The Undertaker and Austin are classic American tough guys. In many ways, the "American badass" is a lot like Terry Funk who was a lot like the TV cowboys of the 1950s. Austin is never afraid to mix it up and grabs a beer when he wins. Maybe when Austin was a kid he never watched the Crusher, but the only two things different between them are the times and the fact that Austin doesn't smoke cigars, as the Crusher did.

Old ideas, new twists

Frank Gotch, Wayne Munn, and Farmer Burns were avowed shooters in the early 1900s. Ninety years later, the WWF promoted the real "Brawl For It All" and some wrestling in Japan sells fans the notion that their matches are real. Chris Benoit, Little Guido, Tazz, and Ken Shamrock utilize submissions regularly.

High flyers like Edge and Christian or Three Count are simply new versions of the Hart family, who all seemed to borrow something from Frenchman Eduardo Carpentier, who surely owed a debt of thanks to the great 1950s star, Antonino Rocca.

You want hardcore? In 1910, Tom Chaaker died after the beating he took at the hands of Yousouf the Terrible Turk. Twenty years later, Stan Stasiak died after ring injuries against champion Ed Don George in Canada. How's death for hardcore?

Even tag teams have been around for ages. West Coast gold diggers wrestled loggers at the turn of the century. Documents date tag matches back as far as 1901.

Wrestling giants Kevin Nash, Prince Albert, and Kane are large, powerful men. But wasn't Abe Lincoln, one of the first United States champions in 1831, 6-foot-8?

Bill Goldberg had a make-believe winning streak that was nothing short of impressive. When Farmer Burns retired, his record was

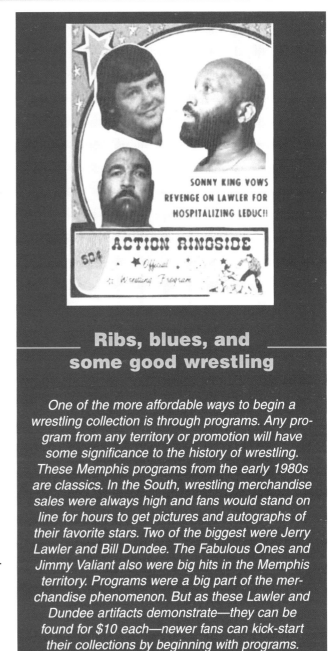

Ribs, blues, and some good wrestling

One of the more affordable ways to begin a wrestling collection is through programs. Any program from any territory or promotion will have some significance to the history of wrestling. These Memphis programs from the early 1980s are classics. In the South, wrestling merchandise sales were always high and fans would stand on line for hours to get pictures and autographs of their favorite stars. Two of the biggest were Jerry Lawler and Bill Dundee. The Fabulous Ones and Jimmy Valiant also were big hits in the Memphis territory. Programs were a big part of the merchandise phenomenon. But as these Lawler and Dundee artifacts demonstrate—they can be found for $10 each—newer fans can kick-start their collections by beginning with programs.

said to be an amazing 6,000 wins and six losses.

The first decade of professional wrestling was spectacular. Certainly, the names are different, but wrestling just has not changed all that much. In the next century, perhaps matches will be held on floating platforms in outer space, but we can always be certain that someone will get drilled with a steel chair.

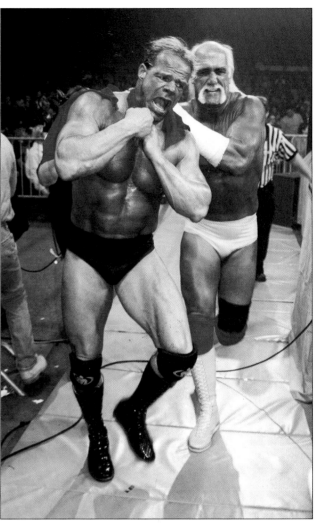

Classic feuds between wrestlers have been ongoing since the dawn of the sport, whether it's Tommy Dreamer and Justin Credible, left; Lex Luger and Hulk Hogan, right; or Ric Flair and Sting, pictured below.

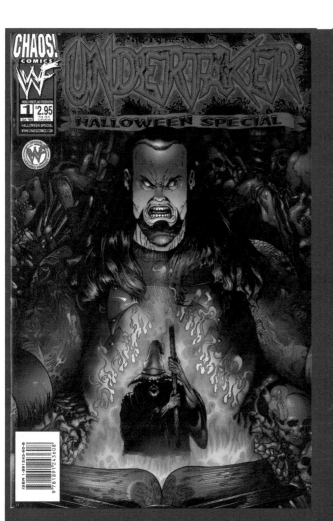

Cartoon characters they were not

Comic books have always been valuable to collectors. In wrestling, several lines of comics have been released in the last few years. The Ultimate Warrior and Kevin Nash have been subjects of a book, and Chaos Comics has developed several lines featuring World Wrestling Federation characters like Chyna, Steve Austin, the Undertaker, and Mankind. This September 1999 special-edition Mankind book and Undertaker Halloween special from October 1999 are found today at increased prices (around $15 each) because stores actually sold out the product. The artwork in the books is comparable to some of the best comic producers.

Chapter 14

The Slamographies

The following is a list of the most notable wrestlers in the world:

A

Abdullah the Butcher and "Maniac" Mark Lewin work over Kevin Sullivan in their corner.

Abdullah the Butcher: This madman from Sudan is a legend and his 400-pound frame and scarred forehead will scare the toughest of fans. Born in Montreal, Abdullah has been all over the world. He did not hold many titles, but never needed to. He was also prone to using a fork on opponents.
Adrian Adonis: Keith Franks had numerous high-profile runs as the East Coast's bad boy. He was a very solid technician whose career took off as Jesse Ventura's tag-team partner in the East-West Connection. Later, an overweight Adonis appeared in the WWF using a flamboyant homosexual gimmick. He died a few years later in a car wreck in Canada, en route to an independent show.

Adrian Adonis, right, with his partner Jesse "The Body" Ventura.

Adrian Baillargeon: From a family of wrestlers in the 1950s and 1960s, he had the flexibility of a rubber band.

Adrian Street: Exotic Adrian was a fine tactical wrestler with an English shooter's background. He borrowed Alice Cooper's gimmick and became a hit. He wrestled in the South, and Gulf Coast areas in the late 1970s and early 1980s, and the face-painted oddity even recorded several albums.

Ahmed Johnson: This large, muscular specimen was a WWF star in early 1990s, he won the I-C title and appeared poised for a world title, but his career dropped fast. Was seen in WCW in 2000.

Aja Kong: Female wrestler from Japan who had some classic bouts in the early 1990s.

Akio Sato: A Japanese star who had success in Central States area, he partnered with Pat Tanaka as the Orient Express in WWF.

Akira Maeda: Bonafide shooter from Japan, he was founder of several overseas groups including UWF.

Al Costello: Was the backbone of the tag team the Fabulous Kangaroos in the 1950s. He later managed the team and drew well in Detroit and Toronto. He generally wrestled as a villain, and became a trainer in the 1980s.

Al Madril: Portland-area funny man who was never far from a witty line, he used old tricks like a chain in the boot or foreign object in the trunks to outwit opponents.

Al Perez: A Latin star, he was a Florida mainstay in the 1980s. He also ventured to the Dallas area and won several regional titles; often had a manager with him.

Al Snow: A WWF goof ball, who can actually wrestle, however. He has gone through many name changes and was once known as Avatar in the WWF. He went psycho at the behest of Paul Heyman in ECW and has been in WWF for several years.

Al Tomko: A British Columbia promoter who also wrestled from the 1960s to 1970s.

Alex Karras: One of the biggest football stars to wear the tights, he called wrestling the "grunt-and-groan circuit." He began his career in a feud with Dick the Bruiser and later, after wrestling, starred in film (most notably Mel Brooks' "Blazing Saddles") and TV ("Webster").

Alex Wright: German phenom who can use the ropes with the best of them. Nicknamed "Das Wunderkind" and has been with WCW through the late 1990s.

Alex Wright.

Alexis Smirnoff: Midwest jobber from the 1980s, who also found wrestling in California.

Alfred Hayes: His Lordship was a WWF announcer through the 1980s and was once a wrestler in the 1960s.

Ali Baba: A real world champion who toured Europe, South Africa, and India, his world-title match with Dick Shikat harkens to the days when fans believed wrestling was real.

Amish Roadkill: A grad of ECW wrestling school and was trained by Tazz. He has a strange gimmick that finally caught on of late: his favorite line is "Chickens!" and no one is sure what that actually means.

Andre the Giant: A legend in wrestling during the 1970s, few wrestlers had more worldwide appeal than Andre. His career climaxed at Wrestlemania III main event in 1987. Was the king of the Battle Royal; he never lost in those matches.

Angel of Death: This bald and menacing wrestler from the 1980s wrestled in Calgary and World Class and won several titles.

Angelo Mosca: King Kong Mosca is one of the Canadian Football League's true legends. A former MVP and Hall of Fame inductee who was a main-event star in the 1970s in both Canada and the U.S., Mosca was comfortable as a heel. He was 270 pounds, 6-3, and looked like a renegade from the HBO show, "The Sopranos."

Angelo Poffo: Father of Randy Savage and Lanny Poffo, he was one of the most well-conditioned athletes of any era and set numerous world records for pushups and sit-ups. Poffo peaked in the 1970s, but wrestled until the 1980s. He was known for founding the ICW in the 1970s and battled for turf in Memphis with rival promoters Nick Gulas and Jerry Jarrett. He folded the group after his sons left for greener pastures.

Animal: One-half of the Road Warriors, this Chicago native trained in Minneapolis and was the stronger, more powerful half of the team. Road Warriors are the most popular tag team ever and has held numerous tag championships.

Antonino Rocca: Was one of the first barefooted wrestlers and a true innovator of aerial maneuvers. He wrestled in the 1950s and 1960s and was a legendary figure in Puerto Rico and on the East Coast. Rocca was one of the few stars who earned the respect of even the most cynical promoters.

Antonio Inoki: Like Giant Baba, he reached legendary status in native Japan and is still going strong in politics and promoting, and operates New Japan wrestling. He was a long-time nemesis of Baba, but the two respected each other tremendously.

Arn Anderson.

Arn Anderson: Marty Lunde was a jobber before he caught on as an "Anderson" and was an integral piece to the Four Horsemen. His small size was outshone by his tremendous interviews and in-ring skills, and has numerous singles and tag titles to his credit.

Arnold Skaaland: Wrestled as the "Golden Boy" in the 1950s through the East and once managed Bob Backlund in WWF.

Art Barr: Portland area son of promoter Sandy Barr, he was very small but was a buzzsaw in the ring. Roddy Piper crowned him with the gimmick Beetlejuice and Barr's career flourished. He was in WCW as The Juicer and hit his stride in Mexico as Eddy Guerrero's partner. He died of heart failure at a young age.

Lovemachine Art Barr.

Asya: A female bodybuilder from WCW who was valet for Ric Flair in late 1990s and often compared to WWF's Chyna.

Atsushi Onita: This crazy Japanese star bled often to gain sympathy with crowds and is a cult hero in Japan. He started the trend of hardcore matches with his promotion, FMW, in the late 1980s.

Austin Idol: Southern star who claims Hulk Hogan stole his gimmick; he was a gifted talker and his match vs. Jerry Lawler in 1987 drew a sell-out to Memphis Coliseum. He never became a national star, but was a super regional performer.

Austin Idol.

Awesome Kongs: This heavy-set tag team, under masks during the early 1990s, wrestled in Dallas but got a huge break in WCW that was short-lived, though.

Axl Rotten: ECW star who teamed with Balls Mahoney in many a hardcore match; not adverse to hitting people with chairs.

Axl Rotten.

B

Baby Doll: Valet of Dusty Rhodes and Tully Blanchard in NWA during the mid-1980s, she was the apple of many men's eyes and patterned her look after rocker Pat Benatar.

Bad Man Jose Quintero: Noted Puerto Rican jobber from the 1960s, who won numerous amateur-night talent contests by singing in broken English.

Bad News Allen Coage: A former Olympic judo team member and top star in Japan in the 1980s. He broke in the sport under the Hart family tutelage and had a successful WWF stint in late 1980s.

Balls Mahoney: Formerly Boo Bradley in Smoky Mountain Wrestling, he patterned his career after Cactus Jack while in ECW for several years. This New Jersey native has been slammed on fire, thumb tacks, and tables.

Balls Mahoney hooks one.

Bam Bam Bigelow: This tattooed bad boy from Asbury Park, N.J. trained under Larry Sharpe. An agile big man, he wrestled in Dallas before heading to WWF in the mid-1980s and still performs regularly.

Barbarian: A three-decade star who is a tall, muscular being, he uses a wild gimmick and is a former tag partner of the Warlord in the Powers of Pain.

Baron Scicluna: A 1960s and 1970s star from the New York area, he held a tag title with Smasher Sloan.

Baron Von Raschke: This former Nebraska wrestling and football star became a menacing "German," after using his real name, Jim Raschke, failed to catch on. He was a singles star throughout the U.S. and also had multiple tag-team partners. He settled in with the AWA and was master of the "claw."

Barry Darsow: He has used many gimmicks and was called Krusher Darsow, Demolition Smash, Repo Man, and Blacktop Bully among others. He is said to have saved his money well. And wrestles on independents.

Barry Horowitz: Noted jobber from the WWF, he always patted himself on the back, but was a talented wrestler, however.

Barry Windham: A second-generation wrestler who won numerous titles with Mike Rotunda, Windham was even an NWA World champion. In his youth, he had the grace of a true technician, despite his 6-7, 270-pound frame. His series with Ric Flair in the 1980s were phenomenal. He is the son of Blackjack Mulligan and older brother of Kendal Windham.

Bart Gunn: One half of the Smoking Gunns team with Billy Gunn, he appeared ready for a career in UFC before Butterbean knocked him unconscious at Wrestlemania. He has been in Japan trying to escape that embarrassment ever since.

Bart Sawyer: A Portland fire plug who is pals with Roddy Piper, he has been to Memphis and got his name after cutting his hair like cartoon kid Bart Simpson.

Bearcat Wright: An African-American pioneer, who broke color barriers to main event in the U.S.

Bearcat Wright.

Bert Prentice: A man of many roles, he has been a promoter, matchmaker, manager, and singer. He has mostly been located in the South and was one-time operator of Music City Wrestling.

Bertha Faye: a.k.a. Rhonda Singh, this rough-and-tumble wrestler has been in Japan most of her career and had a short stint in WWF.

Betty Grable: A famous wrestler of the 1950s and 1960s, she was pretty and talented.

Beulah: A valet in ECW, she left wrestling to earn her college degree and guided Raven and Tommy Dreamer.

Beverly Brothers: Wayne Bloom and Mike Enos were a nice tag team in the mid-1990s and both wrestled as the Destruction Crew in AWA and as the Minnesota Wrecking Crew in WCW before heading to WWF under this name. They parted ways and now wrestle as single's stars.

Big Boss Man: Surprisingly agile, he started as Bubba Rogers, a bodyguard for Jim Cornette, and was offered a deal in WWF as the Boss Man—he has been on national TV ever since.

Big Daddy Siki: Also known as Sweet Daddy Siki, he was one of the first black men to dye his hair blond. Always a showman, he enjoyed music immensely and was most known in Toronto, where he ran a training school through the early 1990s.

Big Van Vader: Leon White, a rugged big man in wrestling, became Vader after floundering in AWA prelims. New Japan and Disney trademarked the name and signature mask that blew smoke as he entered the arena. He once held world titles in four countries simultaneously and had a big run in WCW in the 1990s. Vader toured with WWF for several years and remains an icon in Japan.

Bill Alphonso: A former referee who switched to managing in ECW, he was once the interpreter for El Gigante and has managed Tazz, Sabu, and Rob Van Dam to many titles. He is known to blow his whistle during matches.

Bill Dundee: A former Australian tightrope artist who became a wrestling star in Memphis in late 1970s and early 1980s, he was a longtime foe and friend of Jerry Lawler. He has held numerous mid-South singles and tag titles and his son Jamie is a veteran wrestler. Dundee has been a coordinator behind the scenes and managed WCW stars in the 1990s.

Bill Eadie: A man of many identities, he wrestled as the Masked Superstar, Demolition, and others, but never as Bill. He had the biggest run as one half of Demolition in the WWF.

Bill Irwin: The brother of Scott Irwin, he has been through most major territories and got his start in AWA. He used to wear a cowboy outfit to the ring, and later used a hockey player gimmick named the Goon.

Bill Miller: Wrestled as the mysterious Mr. M during the 1950s and wore a dark mask with an "M" sewn to it. He starred in Midwest rings.

Bill Watts: A rough cowboy from Oklahoma who was a major player in the 1960s. When he retired, he opened Mid South wrestling and later the UWF and was a genius of early 1980s match-making.

Billy Anderson: California-based trainer who has sent his grads to Japan; his most famous grad is Louis Spicolli.

Billy Graham: The Superstar was a former WWF champion and now claims his use of steroids destroyed his health. He was a flamboyant heel during the 1970s and wore tie-dyed shirts.

Billy Gunn.

Billy Gunn: A WWF star, he hit it big as Road Dogg's partner in the New Age Outlaws. He used to be in the Smoking Gunns team, trained in Florida, and is a former tag and I-C champ.

Billy Jack Haynes: Northwest star of late 1970s and early 1980s, he was part of the WWF during its 1980s expansion. He has tried his hand at promoting. He also brought a chain to the ring.

Billy Kidman: This acrobatic star in WCW couldn't reach beyond the cruiserweight level and had many spectacular matches with Rey Mysterio Jr. and Juventud Guerrera.

Billy Robinson: English star of the 1960s and 1970s, wrestled in the AWA, and was a wily veteran in the ring.

Black Bart: A Texas wrestler who wore all black costumes to the ring, he also brought a whip with him; wrestled for WCCW, UWF, and NWA in the 1980s.

Blue Demon: A Mexican superstar from the 1970s, he was a nemesis to Mil Mascaras and wore a blue mask.

Blackjack Mulligan: A big mean Texan at 6-8 and 300 pounds, this black-haired bad guy won numerous tag titles with Blackjack Lanza. The Blackjacks seemed unbeatable in the WWA, with Bobby Heenan as their manager in the 1970s, and they appeared on the Inoki-Ali pay-per-view undercard.

Blue Boy and Jasmin St. Claire.

Blue Meanie: This strange gimmick wrestler found a home in ECW and actually got a shot in WWF. He left wrestling to lose weight and get in shape, and looks better than ever now as the Blue Boy.

Bob Armstrong: This former fireman, who loved wrestling enough to leave a week before his pension was secured, became an icon in the South East. He appeared in NWA rings and on TBS, and is the father of Brad, Steve, and Scott Armstrong.

Bob Backlund: The pride of Princeton, Minneota, he trained in the same school as Jesse Ventura and was WWF champion in the early 1980s. He had epic feuds with Ken Patera and Don Muraco that drew thousands to sell-out bouts at Madison Square Garden.

Bob Caudle: An old-school announcer from the Mid-Atlantic and NWA area during the 1980s.

Bob Geigel: Was a Central States promoter for many years.

Bob Holly: Formerly Sparky Plugg in WWF, he underwent a name change in the late 1990s. Hardcore matches put him on the map and he is now a veteran WWF employee.

Bob Orton Jr.: An underrated technician from the 1980s, he was a consummate tag-team partner and talented enough to be a single's threat. He was part of WWF's explosion in the 1980s and teamed with Roddy Piper and Greg Valentine. He is the son of Bob Orton Sr., who was also known as the Zebra Kid.

Bob Roop: A Southern wrestler from the 1970s, he won many regional titles.

Bob Sweetan: A Central States wrestler from the 1960s and 1970s, he was involved in many bloodbaths.

Bobby Duncum Sr.: A wild man from the 1960s and 1770s, he had long blond hair and was mostly a brawler; was also in AWA.

Bobby Duncum Jr.: Looked and wrestled much like his pop; he died suddenly of heart failure in 1999.

Bobby Eaton: A technically sound wrestler from the 1980s, he was one half of the Midnight Express and was usually the best wrestler wherever he went. He is now a trainer.

Bobby "The Brain" Heenan: The best manager to ever live, he began his career as a

wrestler in Indiana. He used his incredible wit to build up his stable of wrestlers and had a career-long feud with Hulk Hogan.

Bobby Jaggers: A Southern star from the 1980s, he teamed with Dutch Mantell as the Kansas Jayhawks.

Bobo Brazil: An African-American star famous in Detroit for his 1970s' feud with the Sheik, he was very influential for breaking color barriers.

Booker T.: Very gifted and athletic wrestler from WCW. A former world singles and tag champ, he teamed with Stevie Ray as Harlem Heat and has learned his craft well.

Boris Barishnikoff: The early name of WWF tag champion Nikolai Volkoff.

Boris Malenko: A superb technical wrestler and trainer, he is the originator of the Russian chain match and was never shy by

a microphone. His sons, Jody and Dean, also wrestle.

Boris Zukoff: A Russian-gimmick wrestler from the 1980s, he was mainly a jobber and had a strange-looking head.

Brad Armstrong: One of the three sons in the "Armstrong" family, he was a fine technical wrestler who never made it nationally because of his size; regionally, he was a champion in the 1980s.

Brad Rheingans: Prelim wrestler who has been a trainer for 10-plus years, he primarily worked in the Midwest but had stints in Japan.

Bradshaw: West Texas native who harkens the look of Stan Hansen, he played football in college and is a mid-card performer, but has a defined role in WWF. He teams with Farooq as the APA and is known to be a stock trading whiz.

Brady Boone: This talented wrestler, with a myriad of abilities, was very acrobatic and won numerous titles in Portland in the 1980s. He also wrestled under a mask as the Battle Kat in the WWF. He died in a car accident.

Bret Hart: One of the most gifted wrestlers of the modern era, he comes from a wrestling family. He blended a distinct style that combines Japanese wrestling with high flying. Hart took the WWF title and brought respectability back to the belt, but later went to WCW and was misused; he had to retire from post-concussion syndrome.

Brian Adams: A large man from Hawaii, he trained under several top Japanese stars and married Antonio Inoki's daughter. He wrestled in Portland, WCW, and WWF and was the third member of Demolition.

Brian Adias: A wrestler based out of Dallas, he was a star in the early 1980s and a former Texas champ.

Brian Blair: Florida native who was one half of the Killer Bees team, along with Jim Brunzell. He now works for NWA Florida.

Brian Christopher: Real-life son of Jerry Lawler, he has a gift for interviews and is a fun heel. He has been a major star of late as Grand Master Sexay in the WWF. Before that, he toiled through several bad gimmicks.

Brian Hildebrand: A very talented manager and referee who died of cancer in 1999, he was integral behind the scenes at Smoky Mountain Wrestling and some say he was the best referee to ever work.

Brian Lee: A tall and rugged Southern wrestler, he has been in many territories through the South and wrestled as the replacement Undertaker in the early 1990s.

Brian Pillman: Was a top star wherever he went and left a legacy in Stampede, ECW, WWF, and WCW before his death in 1998. He was a former football player at Miami (Ohio) and for NFL's Cincinnati Bengals.

Brian Pillman.

Brickhouse Brown: African-American heel from Memphis who feuded with Jerry Lawler for many years; he also worked in Dallas.

Bronko Lubich: Texas wrestler from the 1960s who later worked in World Class as a referee.

Bronko Nagurski: Former football star turned wrestling world champion from the 1940s and 1950s.

Brother Love: His real name is Bruce Pritchard and he's the brother of wrestler Tom Pritchard. Bruce never wrestled, but was a behind-the-scenes genius and got a chance to be Brother Love in the WWF during the 1990s.

Bruce Hart: Extremely intelligent wrestler who has been the brainchild of many wrestling revolutions, he is credited for bringing the Japanese style to North America. He operated Calgary Stampede for many years and teamed with Brian Pillman in late 1980s.

Bruise Brothers: These twins wrestled in many areas in the 1990s and were seen in Memphis, Portland, WWF, and WCW.

Bruiser Brody: One of the hardcore innovators, no fan or wrestler was safe when the 6-8 longhaired wildman was around. He once had a 60-minute draw with then-NWA champion Ric Flair and is a legend, even after his death, in Japan. Brody also had legendary matches with Inoki, and teamed with Jimmy Snuka and Stan Hansen. He was slain in 1988, in Puerto Rico.

Bruno Sammartino: One of the true legends of wrestling, he sold out Madison Square Garden over a five- to 10-year span. A strongman who is known to take his wrestling and legacy quite seriously, Sammartino was a franchise of the WWF for most of the 1960s to mid-1970s.

Brute Bernard: One of the first big bad bald men, he teamed with Skull Murphy and was a main-event star of the 1950s and 1960s.

Buck Zumhoff: One of the first wrestlers to use ring entrance music, he brought a boom box to the ring. He was in the AWA and World Class in the 1980s and is still active in Midwest.

Buddy Landell: Southern performer who used a Nature Boy gimmick, he honorably battled back from drug abuse and was a regional champ in the 1980s and 1990s.

Buddy Rogers: Was the first WWWF champion from the 1960s and also a former NWA champion; he used the name "Nature Boy."

Buddy Roberts: Best known for his tag-team work, he teamed first with Jerry Brown as the Hollywood Blonds, and then with Gordy and Hayes as the Freebirds.

Buddy Rose: A noted mid-card performer from the late 1970s and 1980s, he was a very talented worker and lives in Portland.

Buff Bagwell: A Georgia native who blossomed in the 1990s, he started as the Handsome Stranger in Global Wrestling and moved to WCW as Marcus Alexander. Bagwell is a is former WCW tag champ and runs a wrestling novelty store.

Bugsy McGraw: A Florida gimmick wrestler from the 1970s and 1980s, he teamed with Jimmy Valiant and Dusty Rhodes and was in NWA briefly.

Bull Buchanan: WWF mid-card wrestler and member of the Truth Commission and RTC, he has good agility for big man.

Bulldog Brower: One of the best brawlers of the 1960s and 1970s, he played the role of a lunatic.

Bushwackers: Formerly the Sheepherders from New Zealand; as the Sheepherders, Butch Miller and Luke Williams were blood lusting mad men, then the WWF came calling. As the Bushwackers, they toned down and became family friendly funny men.

Butch Reed: Former rodeo star turned wrestler, he used the nickname Hacksaw and the Natural, and teamed with Ron Simmons in WCW as Doom.

Buzz Sawyer: An energetic and fast-paced performer, he had his best years in Georgia in the early 1980s.

C

Canadian Wolfman: He lived to train bears and promote outlaw cards in Canada, and died in a car accident with Adrian Adonis.

Carlos Colon: A Puerto Rico icon from the 1960s to 1990s, he was the island's mainstay for many years. He never was popular in the U.S., but was still a multi-time WWC champ. His son Carly is now wrestling.

Chad Brock: A former Power-Plant trainee, who had hits on the country charts in 1999.

Chavo Guerrero: Former Texas champion who was popular among Latino fans in U.S. border towns, he was a talented high flyer and had success in Mid-South territory.

Chavo Guerrero Jr., far right, with his fellow Misfits in Action: Lash LeRoux, A-Wall and General Rection.

Chavo Guerrero Jr.: Is a cruiserweight champion from WCW and related to the famous Guerrero family. He has been a member of MIA for nearly a year.

Chaz: Has been many characters in WWF: a Headbanger, a Beaver Cleaver wanna-be, a party animal and a Sheik. He started in SMW.

Chief Don Eagle: One of the sport's true American Indians, he appeared in the U.S. and Canada in the 1950s and 1960s and was also popular in England.

Chigusa Nagayo: A Japanese female champion who had a big feud with Madusa Micelli in late 1980s, she is one of the most popular females ever in Japan.

Chris Adams: This superb English wrestler was a star in Dallas in the early 1980s as the partner of Gino Hernandez. He wrestled in Japan and WCW and used the superkick. He is known best for training Steve Austin.

Chris Benoit: A believable wrestler from Canada, he trained under the Hart family tutelage and is a former WCW world champ. He also won the WWF I-C title and has had many five-star bouts in Calgary and Japan.

Chris Benoit, left, hangs out with Chris Jericho pre-show.

Chris Candido and Tammy Sytch.

Chris Candido: This former NWA champion from the East Coast had shots in Smoky Mountain, WCW, and WWF. He's married to Tammy Sytch and was member of the Body Donnas team with Tom Pritchard. He is now with XPW.

Chris Champion: Memphis wrestler who was part of the New Breed team, he once wrestled as the Ninja Turtle.

Chyna is a character on the edge

Like many stars of the World Wrestling Federation, Chyna's stardom has reached far beyond the ring. Trained by Killer Kowalski, Chyna was a big reason for the WWF's success in the late 1990s. She parlayed her success into numerous TV roles, an exercise video, and a new book. Advertisers see her as a unique pitch woman. RC Cola used Chyna, Steve Austin, the Rock, and Edge in a 2000 ad campaign for Edge cola. Four posters were made with each wrestler's likeness and given away as a promotion. Today, the posters are not expensive to buy or trade. Ads with wrestlers in them have always shown to be sought-after collectibles.

Chris Chetti: Cousin of Tazz and a grad of ECW school, he teamed with Nova and tours around the East Coast.

Chris Daniels: An East Coast independent wrestler, he uses the name Fallen Angel and wrestles in Japan as Curry Man. He has also been to WCW.

Chris Daniels headlocks Suicide Kid.

Chris Jericho: Canadian star who is often compared with Roddy Piper, he is small but an excellent technician. He won the WWF title on RAW, but the decision was reversed. He is now a major star in WWF. His father is a former pro hockey player.

Chris Jericho asks a photographer who the man is.

Chris Taylor: A 400-plus-pound former Olympic wrestler, who allegedly signed a million-dollar deal with the AWA in the 1970s, he died at the age of 30 before hitting his stride.

Chris Von Erich: The smallest and youngest of the family that seemed to be jinxed, he committed suicide after an aborted attempt to follow his brothers and father in the ring.

Christian: Another Canadian independent star who got a shot in WWF, he is one of the more talented workers found today. He is multiple tag champ with Edge and started in the WWF as part of the Brood.

Christian York: Partner of Joey Mathews in ECW tag team, he has potential to be a star one day.

Chuck Palumbo: This Power Plant grad had a feud with Lex Luger in WCW and has teamed with Sean Stasiak and Sean O'Hare.

Chyna in her Degeneration X days, with X-Pac and Triple H.

Chyna: WWF's biggest female star ever, she is the first woman to win the I-C title and is a consummate pro in and out of the ring. She wrote a book about her life and was an integral member of the original Degeneration X.

Col. DeBeers: Portland-based wrestler who used a racist, South African gimmick in the 1980s.

Cora Combs: Second-generation female star from the 1970s.

Cousin Luke: Saddled with a hillbilly gimmick his whole career, he was in WWF during the early 1980s.

Cpl. Kirschner: A mildly talented wrestler from the 1980s, he was in WWF briefly and still wrestles, mostly overseas, using the name John Rambo.

Craig Pittman: Was known as the sergeant and wore fatigues in the ring. WCW was his home during the mid-1990s.

Crash Holly: West-Coast independent wrestler who, despite his small frame, reached fame in the WWF.

Crash Holly.

Crash: Begrudgingly works as a hardcore wrestler.

Crusher: Innovator of the stomach claw and bolo punch, this barrel-chested brawler drove fans wild in the 1950s and 1960s. He later became a popular fan favorite and is known most for his trademark cigars and hilarious interviews.

Crusher Jerry Blackwell: One of the few big men who could move well in the ring, he neared 400 pounds and preferred to bleed and brawl. He once drove a nail through a 2 x 4 with his forehead.

Crybaby Cannon: George Cannon was a wrestler, manager, announcer, and promoter and is best known for his work in Detroit's Big Time Wrestling. He got his nickname from "crying" after losses.

Curtis Thompson: Muscled independent wrestler who has been in Memphis and Portland, he was in WCW as Firebreaker Chip.

Cyrus: A trained wrestler who has been mostly used as a manager, he was in WWF briefly as manager of the Oddities and has been in ECW the last year.

D

Dan Hodge: Legendary Oklahoma wrestler, he was a champion light heavyweight of the 1950s and the first wrestler to grace the cover of *Sports Illustrated*.

Dan Kroffat: Wrestler in Canada and Japan who teamed with Doug Furnas, he was in WWF as Phil Lafon in the early 1990s.

Dan Severn: Ultimate shoot-fighter who crossed over to pro wrestling, he is a submission specialist and had great "real" matches in UFC with Ken Shamrock.

Danno O'Mahoney: Former world champ in the 1930s, his two wins over Jim Londos and Ed Don George solidified him as champion.

Danny Davis: A small wrestler who was a member of the Nightmares with Ken Wayne during the 1980s, he now runs OVW and a camp in Indiana.

Danny Spivey: Very tall wrestler who has had trips to WCW and WWF, he teamed with Mike Rotunda and Sid.

Dave Brown: A 25-plus-year commentator for Memphis wrestling, he has survived many different management changes. This class act is actually a local weatherman.

Dave Taylor: English wrestler from the 1980s and 1990s, he was once a partner of Steven Regal's in WCW.

Davey Boy Smith: Ushered in a new high-risk style in the early 1980s as a high-flying 160-pound wrestler. He later became a strongman as a member of the British Bulldogs and was a major player in WWF and WCW in the 1980s and 1990s.

Davey Boy Smith, in his British Bulldog days, tries the Bo Derek "10" look.

David Flair: Real-life son of Ric Flair, he was pushed into the limelight before he was ready and has been learning his craft in NWA Wildside.

David Sammartino: Son of Bruno, he was unfairly pushed to live up to his father's legendary status. In his own right, he was a decent wrestler, but got burned out on the sport before he hit his stride.

David Schultz: A trucker and bounty hunter before wrestling, this classic territory wrestler worked a major program with Hulk Hogan in the AWA in the 1980s and played the role of a redneck bully. He lost a lawsuit to journalist John Stossel, whom he hit during a TV special.

David Von Erich: Probably the most talented of the Von Erich sons, he looked to be poised for an NWA title reign when he died suddenly in Japan of toxic shock syndrome at age 25.

Dean Malenko: A master of submission moves and counter holds, his tough TV personality is not far from his real-life persona. He had great matches in Japan and is a former WCW cruiser champ.

——————— Hmmm, ———————
shaking the ropes and wearing face paint makes you a Warrior?

In the early 1990s, wrestling was looking for its next star. Hulk Hogan's yellow-tights era was coming to a close. Lex Luger and Sting were anointed the next generation in WCW, but the WWF had to find a new star of its own. They eventually grabbed Jim Hellwig from the Dallas area, who was toiling as the Dingo Warrior in World Class Wrestling. The WWF kept his face paint, added some colorful twists to his outfit and made him the Ultimate Warrior. The gimmick was a huge success. Soon enough, the Warrior was given the torch to be the next WWF champion. As a wrestler, Hellwig was lost; but as a showman, he had appeal. It was a relatively short title reign, but his impact is still felt. An LJN doll in his likeness was released and has since become one of the most sought-after dolls in wrestling collectibles. A mint-on-card Warrior doll can fetch up to $300. Not bad for a guy with a $10 ring costume.

Debra and Jeff Jarrett.

Debra: Former wife of Steve McMichael, she recently married Steve Austin and is a valet and manager. She claims she was destined to be a star on TV.

Del Wilkes: A well-sculpted wrestler who used different gimmicks like the Trooper and the Patriot. He had a shot in the WWF, but suffered an injury and had to retire shortly thereafter.

Dennis Condrey: A former partner in the Midnight Express with Bobby Eaton and Randy Rose.

Destroyer: Dick Beyers was an amateur standout at Syracuse and became a famed masked man. He was a big star in Japan in the 1960s and remains a legend there. He feuded with Fred Blassie and John Tolos, among others.

Devon Storm: This East Coast independent star is very acrobatic and has been in WCW for the past year as Crowbar, but was released.

DC Drake: East Coast independent wrestler in the 1980s who used a Mad Dog-type gimmick.

Diamond Dallas Page: Miraculous person who started as a manager, but trained to become a valuable asset in WCW. This former world champ managed Badd Company in AWA and Scott Hall in WCW. He is a native of Florida and wrote a book about his life.

Dick the Bruiser: Rugged ex-football player from the 1950s and 1960s who often partnered with the Crusher through the Midwest.

This cover-up was a big hit

The publishers of TV Guide hit on something special when they capitalized on professional wrestling in the late 1990s. On several occasions, the magazine sold special four-issue sets featuring the likes of Steve Austin and the Undertaker. In fact, TV Guide has used wrestling many times in the past. During the 1950s, stars regularly made its covers. In August 2000, another four-issue set was released featuring the Kat, Kurt Angle, Rikishi, and Chris Jericho. Sold together, the set has greater value than when sold separately. The set is still young, but TV Guides have always shown to be valuable collectibles in time. Add the element of wrestling and a winner is born.

Havoc was his middle name and he died during a work out after his career was over.

Dick Dudley: This large man was once partners with the Dudley Boys in ECW and now wrestles in California.

Dick Hutton: NCAA wrestling standout from the 1960s.

Dick Murdoch: A real take-no-prisoners tough guy, he was the partner of Dusty Rhodes and the two were inseparable and seemingly unbeatable as the Texas Outlaws. He was a main-event star in Japan, U.S., and Puerto Rico in the 1970s and 1980s.

Dick Shikat: Early wrestling star who had a legendary feud with Ali Baba in the 1920s.

Dick Slater: Southern wrestler who teamed with Dick Murdoch and Dusty Rhodes, he was in the WWF briefly in the mid-1980s and toured Japan often.

Dino Bravo: Famed Canadian star from the 1980s, he wrestled in the WWF and was murdered at age 44 in Quebec.

Dirty Dick Raines: Main-event star throughout the U.S. during the 1950s and 1960s, he was always on the brink of stardom. He wrestled during a time when having the nickname "Dirty" was enough to rile fans.

Dirty White Boy: This Kentucky and Alabama-based wrestler has been a road warrior for 20-plus years. He teamed with Lynn Denton as the Dirty White Boys in the early 1980s and was a star in the Smoky Mountain group.

Disqo: Formerly Disco Inferno, he is said to be a creative writer behind the scenes in WCW and was a member of the Filthy Animals.

Dizzy Ed Boulder: a.k.a. Brutus Beefcake, he began as Hulk Hogan's cousin in Florida. A well-built star who reached his peak as Beefcake, he is a former WWF tag champ with Greg Valentine, and later was in WCW as the Zodiac and the Disciple.

D-Lo Brown: Was a member of the Gangstas in the early 1990s with New Jack and Mustafa and has been with WWF for several years. This former European champ looked to break out as part of Nation of Domination, but never did.

D-Lo Brown, left, with Al Snow and Val Venis.

Don Jardine: Best known as the Masked Spoiler, he was a mid-Atlantic mainstay in the 1970s.

Don Kernodle: A Carolinas star from the 1970s, he teamed with Sgt. Slaughter in the NWA.

Don Leo Jonathan: A very athletic big man, the 270-pound Canadian was adept at technical wrestling and brawling and was a major player in the 1950s.

Don Muraco: Started as a Tom Selleck copy from Hawaii and was a fan fave in the 1970s. He turned rulebreaker and bulked up considerably and became filled with abrasive attitude as a heel. He also won the WWF Intercontinental title.

Don Owens: Portland-area promoter for 30-plus years.

Dory Dixon: A former Mr. Universe, he was an African-American pioneer and had his best years in the 1960s.

Dory Funk: Father of Terry and Dory Jr., he was a Texas star in the 1950s and 1960s.

Dory Funk Jr.: Former NWA champ and brother of Terry, he was a master of the spinning toe hold. He proudly defended titles the world over and now runs a training camp in Florida.

Doug Furnas: Former Continental wrestling star from the 1980s, he teamed with Dan Kroffat in Japan.

Doug Gilbert: Son of former wrestler Tommy Gilbert, he pops up in Memphis every year or so and is mainly a brawler.

Doug Somers: Early 1980s performer who was an AWA tag champion with Buddy Rose, he had great matches with the Midnight Rockers.

Downtown Bruno: A pal of Jerry Lawler who got a chance to manage in Memphis, he worked in WWF as Harvey Wippleman and managed Sid at his height of popularity.

Dr. Tom Pritchard: Consummate tag wrestler who is now a talent coordinator for the WWF.

Ohio Valley Wrestling and THORNTON'S Quick Cafe & Market and DUNKIN' DONUTS — CHRISTMAS CHAOS — Louisville Gardens • December 13, 2000 7:30 p.m. — A Stone Cold Christmas!

Ohio Valley Wrestling and 100.5 The FOX present the ROCKIN' RUMBLE — Louisville Gardens • Friday, June 23, 2000 — KANE — MANKIND — Win A Prize With The Lucky Number! Nº 01286

Who were they expecting? Santa "Claws?"

When Jim Cornette joined forces with former wrestler "Nightmare" Danny Davis in Ohio Valley Wrestling in 1998, a new era was born. Since then, Cornette has helped develop OVW, based out of Louisville, into one of the country's premiere training grounds. A working relationship with the World Wrestling Federation has not hurt. The WWF sends OVW its up and coming stars to gain experience before live crowds. A year to 18 months later, those youngsters are ready for prime time. In turn, the WWF has been sending OVW major stars—like Steve Austin and the Hardy Boys—to wrestle on marquee shows, like the Rockin' Rumble and Christmas Chaos shows. This program can sell for close to $20. Kane, Chris Benoit, and Lita were just some of the stars that were signed to perform. Cornette, who began his career in the days of "territories," has tried to bring that way of promoting back to life. Videos, autographs, and programs are a way fans all around the country can join in on the fun in Louisville.

Dr. X: Midwest masked star from the 1960s, his real name was Guy Taylor. He died in the ring in 1968

Droz: This former football player turned wrestler, whose real name is Darren Drozdov, was paralyzed in a freak wrestling accident in 1999. He was nicknamed Puke and still works for WWF.

Duane Gill: A noted jobber who was given TV time in the late 1990s for his impression of Goldberg, the WWF named him "Gillberg."

Dudley Boys: A strange gimmick team dreamed up by Paul Heyman that works, for some reason, the Boys are multiple ECW tag champs. D-Von and Bubba Ray are obviously not related, but they have become stars in WWF and have also won tag titles there.

Duke Droese: Florida-based, he was in WWF in the mid-1990s and was nicknamed the "Dumpster."

Dump Matsumoto: A large Japanese female star who enjoyed using garbage cans to level opponents, she worked in the U.S. in the mid-1980s for WWF.

Dustin Rhodes: Son of Dusty Rhodes, he has been through several name changes, was a credible wrestler in WCW and even won a U.S. title. He went to WWF as the strange Goldust and actually played the part well enough to win the I-C title. He has been back with WCW of late.

Dusty Rhodes: A main-event star in every group he ever appeared in through the 1970s, he became an icon in Florida and NWA and is a three-time NWA champ. He is known for the bionic elbow and witty mannerisms.

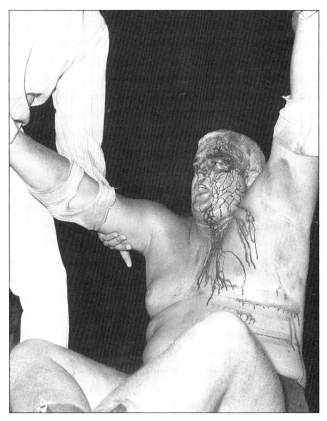

A bloodied Dusty Rhodes, after a match with Danny Hodge and Red Lyons.

Dutch Mantel: A Southern wrestler from the 1970s and 1980s, he had big feuds with Jerry Lawler and Bill Dundee. He has been in NWA, WCW, and WWF and still often works in Puerto Rico.

Dynamite Kid: This high-flying suplex machine was unafraid to hurt his body in the ring. He was a star in Canada and Japan before teaming with Davey Boy Smith in WWF during the 1980s and is a WWF tag champion. He sadly ended his career crippled from the punishment he inflicted on himself and penned the fabulous book, *Pure Dynamite.*

E

Earl Caddock: An early 1900s world champion who won the belt from Joe Stecher.

Earl Maynard: Another bodybuilder who was a hit in the 1960s.

Earthquake: His real name is John Tenta and he was a very large man who wrestled as the Shark and Golga.

Eddie Gilbert: This second-generation star was a major player backstage and is remembered for his creativity in script-writing. He died at age 33 in Puerto Rico.

Eddie Guerrero: A very talented high flyer and former WCW cruiserweight champ, he won the WWF I-C title. He is part of the Radicalz and established himself in Mexico and ECW.

Eddie Guerrero.

Eddie Graham: Noted "brother" of Luke Graham and Billy Graham, he won numerous tag titles in WWF before settling in Florida as a promoter. He committed suicide in the 1980s.

Eddy Mansfield: A renegade wrestler from the 1970s and 1980s, his claim to fame is revealing on TV that wrestling was fake.

Edge: Canadian star who trained with Dory Funk Jr., he is a WWF star of the future. A former tag-team champion with Christian, he is a very charismatic fellow.

Ed Sharkey: A top light heavyweight from the 1960s in the Midwest, he is most noted for training Jesse Ventura, Rick Rude, and the Road Warriors.

Eduardo Carpentier: This high-flying Canadian is said to be related to a boxing family in France. A star of the 1950s and 1960s, he got extra mileage from managing Andre the Giant.

El Canek: Mexican star who was one of the few to actually pin Andre the Giant, he was a popular masked man and toured Japan in the 1960s and 1970s.

El Gigante: An immensely tall foreign wrestler and former basketball player, he joined WCW and later went to WWF as Giant Gonzales.

Elizabeth: Was one-time wife of Randy Savage and played the perfect role of helpless female always in the way of trouble.

Miss Elizabeth and Randy Savage.

El Santo: Mexican movie legend who appeared in more than 80 films, this masked hero rivaled Blue Demon in the ring and out through the 1960s and remains an icon.

Emil Dupree: Longtime Canadian promoter of Maritimes wrestling from the 1950s to 1980s.

Equalizer: Portland area big man who wrestled in WCW as Evad Sullivan.

Eric Bischoff: Former AWA ad salesman turned major power broker in WCW, he is credited for wrestling popularity in the 1990s.

Erik Watts: This second-generation star is the son of Bill Watts and was pushed into limelight before he was ready. He starred in WCW in the early 1990s and was part of WWF's Techno Team 2000.

Erin O'Grady: A West Coast independent wrestler who, despite his small frame, reached fame in the WWF as Crash Holly and begrudgingly works as a hardcore wrestler.

Ernest Miller: An accomplished black belt, he used to compete in karate and kick-boxing events. He is nicknamed The Cat and has been a big part of WCW the last few years.

Ernest Roeber: Christened champion by William Muldoon in 1892, he held the title for several years and battled Yousouf the Turk.

Ernie Ladd: A huge 6-7 African-American wrestler who reached prominence in the NFL, he toured the world through the 1970s and won numerous regional titles, including the mid-south area. He later managed.

Evan Karagis: This WCW cruiserweight was involved with Madusa in storylines and is a member of 3-Count.

Everett Marshall: A former NWA champion robbed of fame, due to injuries suffered in a car accident.

EZ Money: Wrestled in the Southeast for many years and went to ECW and got national exposure. He is a talented rope-to-rope wrestler and knows innovative, eye-popping moves. He recently went to WCW.

F

A referee raises the hand of former world champion, Fabulous Moolah, as her business partner, Mae Young, watches proudly.

Fabulous Moolah: A six-decade women's champ, she had to fight state laws for the right to wrestle. The queen of women wrestlers, this former WWF champion began as a valet named Slave Girl.

Fantastics: Tommy Rogers and Bobby Fulton were a top team in the 1980s and the former UWF tag champs were skilled technicians. They had bloody feuds with Sheepherders.

Farmer Burns: Championed a new age in wrestling when Greco-Roman and collar-and-elbow merged. He was the mentor of the one and only Frank Gotch and claimed to have more than 6,000 wins.

Fit Finlay: An English wrestler who is called a "stretcher," this very rugged wrestler fought back from a devastating knee injury suffered in a hardcore bout.

Frenchy Martin: Canadian manager who was in WWF in the mid-1980s as Dino Bravo's guide.

Flash Flannagan: An Ohio Valley star looking to break-out, he is an awesome hardcore risk-taker and has been to Memphis.

Francine: ECW's Queen of Extreme, she is the gal pal of Tommy Dreamer and has managed Shane Douglas and Justin Credible.

Francine with Shane Douglas.

Frank Baillargeon: This Canadian strongman was the first of four wrestling brothers. Legend has it he was discovered by Verne Gagne while carrying a sick cow on the side of the road.

Frank Gotch: Arguably the greatest technician and pure wrestler to ever live, this Humboldt, Iowa native knew hundreds of holds and was the world champ who beat George Hackenschmidt in a three-hour duel. He died before reaching his prime.

Frank Townsend: A pre-television star who gave world champions a run for their money, he is said to have wrestled in six-hour matches.

Fred Blassie: In-ring star through the 1970s, he is best known as a silver-haired manager who called foes "pencil-necked geeks." He was named the "Vampire" in Japan for his penchant for biting opponents and was a top draw in Los Angeles in the 1960s.

Freddy Miller: A noted Georgia wrestling announcer on WTBS' superstation from the 1970s to 1980s, he coined the phrase, "Be there!" when hyping upcoming shows.

Fritz Von Erich: He had five children who became wrestlers, and he used a German gimmick and the Claw hold. He ran World Class in the early 1980s, using his sons as stars. His real name was Adkisson.

G

Gama Singh: He was one of many Singhs to tour in North America.

Gangrel: David Heath has had many gimmicks and has wrestled in Japan. He was in Memphis as Vampire Warrior, and his Gangrel character was very unique.

Gangrel, with his wife Luna and family dog.

Gary Albright: Former AAU wrestler who starred in Japan in the 1990s, he was related to the Anoia family by marriage before he died suddenly in 1999 from a heart attack.

Gary Hart: An ex-wrestler who reached stardom as a manager in Florida, Dallas, and the NWA, he had a classic feud with Dusty Rhodes over the years.

Gary Young: Texas and Mid-South mid-card star who won regional titles through the 1980s, he is most known for a feud with Eric Embry in Dallas.

Gene Kiniski: Former world champion from the 1960s, he defeated Lou Thesz in St. Louis in 1966 for the belt.

Gene LeBelle: Noted judo star, wrestler, referee, promoter, author, and trainer, he was in numerous films in the 1950s and 1960s and is a California legend.

Gene Okerlund: One of the most recognizable wrestling announcers of the modern era, he was nicknamed Mean Gene. He started in the AWA, but quickly moved to WWF and later WCW. He once wrestled Bobby Heenan and won.

Gene Okerlund interviews a towering Sid.

Gene Stanlee: Noted tag-team partner of brother Steve during the 1950s.

General Adnan Al-Kaissey: Legitimate Iraqi native who played up his connection to Saddam Hussein in storylines, he was a talented amateur wrestler and began as Billy White Wolf. He managed in AWA and later the WWF as Sgt. Slaughter's evil mentor, and once operated a Minneapolis deli.

George Gordienko: A strong Canadian shooter who was respected by his peers.

George Hackenschmidt: In 1905, this German phenom was the world Greco-Roman champ. His match with Frank Gotch was for the undisputed world title, which

Gotch won. Hackenschmidt was a very talented wrestler in his day.

George South: Noted Southern states jobber from NWA and Mid-Atlantic areas, he now runs an Evangelist wrestling promotion that conducts sermons between matches.

George Steele: Used the nickname "Animal" throughout his career and was a WWF draw in the 1970s. He struck fear with audiences by eating turnbuckles and showing his green-colored tongue.

George Tragos: The esteemed mentor of Lou Thesz in the 1920s and 1930s.

Giant Haystacks: One of England's top draws through the 1980s, he weighed nearly 500 pounds.

Giant Shohei Baba: A true legend in Japan, his height was revered and he wrestled from the 1960s to the 1990s. He held the NWA title and won numerous world titles in Japan. He died in 1999 of cancer.

Gino Hernandez: Phenomenally gifted athlete who died in his prime in the early 1980s. He was a collegiate football star and his flamboyant style wowed fans in Dallas.

Godfather: Another wrestler with multiple personalities, he was Papa Shango, the Soul Taker, and Kama before he was the Godfather. His wife used to make his trademark eyeglasses as the non-RTC character. He lives in Las Vegas.

Goldberg: This former pro-football player was urged by Lex Luger and Sting to try wrestling and, to everyone's surprise, his popularity skyrocketed for WCW. He won the world title from Hulk Hogan in his first year and his storylines claimed he had a 175-match win streak. He has slowed down recently while fighting injuries, but can he once again be the phenom he was?

Gordon Solie: Often called the dean of wrestling announcers, he died in 2000 and was most known for his days in Florida and the NWA. This grizzly throated announcer was a tremendous influence on Jim Ross.

Gorgeous George: One of the first multimedia stars of the TV era of the 1950s, he had dyed platinum blond hair and took flamboyance to unseen heights.

Gorilla Monsoon: Former wrestler of the 1960s and 1970s, who later was broadcaster for WWF. He weighed 300 pounds but was a fine amateur wrestler and highly respected, even after his passing.

Gory Guerrero: Legendary father of the Guerrero family and papa of Hector, Mando, and Chavo, he was a noted star in the Southwest.

Grand Wizard: A WWF manager in the 1970s, he always wore sunglasses and a turban. He managed many champions and was well liked backstage.

Great Muta: Keiji Mutoh wowed crowds when he arrived in the U.S. in 1988 and brought the Moonsault with him from Japan. He had a memorable feud with Sting and has been very popular in Japan since then. He now uses his real name.

Great Sasuke: Tremendous high flyer from Japan, he runs Michinoku Pro Wrestling and his career highlight was the 1995 Super Junior tournament.

Greg Gagne: A second-generation star who teamed with Jim Brunzell as the popular High Flyers in the 1980s, he was a classic technician who stuck to the basics.

Greg Valentine: Son of 1960s star Johnny Valentine, he had a bloody feud with Roddy Piper and eventually became a top star in the WWF through the 1980s. He was Intercontinental champ and a tag champ with Brutus Beefcake.

Grizzly Smith: Father of Jake Roberts, Sam Houston, and Rockin' Robin, he was a member of the Kentuckians in the 1960s with Luke Brown. He later worked as a road agent for WCW.

Gus Sonnenberg: A Larry Zbyszko-looking wrestler, he helped solidify wrestling's image in the 1920s.

Gypsy Joe: Namesake of many regional wrestlers during the 1970s.

Haku: A multi-talented man with many identities, over the past 25 years he has wrestled as King Tonga, the Islander, the Tongan Warrior, and Meng. He was considered one of the truly tough men in wrestling.

Happy Humphrey: At 720 pounds, he was the heaviest wrestler to step in the ring and wrestled in the 1950s.

Hard Boiled Haggerty: This big, bald warrior parlayed his AWA talent as a mid-level star of the 1950s and 1960s into a Hollywood career.

Harley Race: This Kansas City native and former classy NWA champion has been wrestling since the 1950s. He has been all over the world and for a time, he was the identity of the NWA. He used a King character in WWF later in his career and is now retired.

Harold Sakata: The original "Odd Job" who appeared in the James Bond film

"Goldfinger." Many Asian stars copied his persona by wearing a top hat and tuxedo.

Hawk: One half of the Road Warriors, he is really from Minneapolis and trained with Animal, Rick Rude, and Nikita Koloff. He was a better wrestler than his partner, had a great gift of gab and was once called Headsick Hegstrand.

Hayabusa: Formerly a masked Japanese star with a flair for the air, he has been unmasked in recent years and is now simply known as "H." He wrestled for ECW and was a main character in FMW. He has been in many exploding ring matches.

Headhunters: A very heavy tag team that won titles in Japan and Mexico, they actually worked in WWF for a few weeks during the mid-1990s.

Hector Guerrero: An acrobatic Latino star, he wrestled mainly in the Southeast U.S. and was Lazer Tron in the NWA. He was also the WWF's Gobbledy Gooke, but he's still trying to forget that chapter in his life.

Hercules: A Florida wrestler with broad shoulders and a mean look, he went to WWF and was a mid-card mainstay. He was also teamed with Paul Roma.

Hercules Ayala: This Puerto Rican heel challenger to hero Carlos Colon in WWC was a very large wrestler with lots of power moves.

Hercules Cortez: One of the strongest and most muscular wrestlers from the 1960s, he won numerous tag-team titles. He was killed in a car accident in Minnesota.

Hillbilly Jim: A gentle-hearted big man who was a comedy act in the WWF during the 1980s.

Hiro Hase: A Japanese star during the 1980s, he was brought to Canada to train with Hart family and won numerous titles in Japan.

Honkytonk Man: Wayne Ferris is a Memphis area legend who borrowed from Elvis Presley's legacy. He failed with attempts at stardom as the Moondog, but

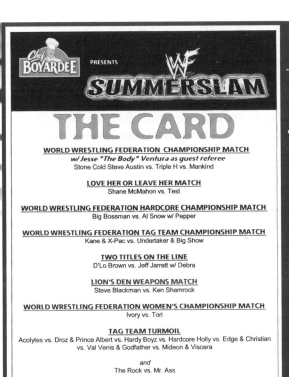

Only one man could control this match

Jesse Ventura said he shocked the world when he became a governor in 1999. Later that year, he shocked the world again when he became the first elected public official to referee a championship wrestling match. The event was Summerslam '99 in Jesse's hometown of Minneapolis. The match, a three-way dance for the World Wrestling Federation title, pit Steve Austin, Mankind, and Triple H against each other. Bits and pieces of memorabilia can be found from that night and this line-up card has been selling for $25. The night was special outside of Jesse's position—Mankind went on to win his third and final WWF world title before retiring.

with the Elvis gimmick, he was a main event star in the WWF and won numerous titles. He's a real-life cousin of Jerry Lawler.

Horst Hoffman: A very talented European shooter who was feared and jeered by fans in the 1970s, he was partner of Baron Von Raschke.

Hugh Morrus: A stocky brawler from WCW, he also wrestled as Capt. Rection. Jim Duggan passed his torch to Morrus in storylines and, indeed, Morrus does bear a resemblance to Duggan.

Hugo Savinovich: Famed Puerto Rican wrestler, manager and promoter, he has settled in as a liaison between the WWF and the island. He was also a Spanish announcer for WWF.

Hulk Hogan, in his "Hollywood" days, battles Sting.

Hulk Hogan: A true superstar in wrestling behind the WWF, he became a household name in the 1980s and 1990s. He is a former WCW and WWF champ and revitalized wrestling with the NWO in the mid-1990s. Many fans have gotten interested in wrestling by watching Hogan.

Hunter Hearst Helmsley: Major star for the WWF and former world champion, he was a member of the revolutionary group Degeneration X. Trained by Killer Kowalski, he started as Terra Rising and was in WCW before WWF.

I

Iceman Parsons: African-American star who received international exposure in the 1980s, he is best known for his work in Bill Watts' UWF and World Class.

Igor: Polish strongman who starred in the AWA, Puerto Rico, and the rebellious IWA in the 1970s.

The mighty Igor was known to break bricks over his head.

Illio DiPaolo: A mid-card wrestler from the East Coast in the 1950s, he was later promoted.

Iron Mike Sharpe: Son of Ben, he often toured Canada but was best known for his work as a WWF jobber in the 1980s.

Iron Sheik: Iranian-born Kosrow Vasari was once said to have been a bodyguard for the Shah. He had a strong amateur wrestling background, was also a weight lifter and became a controversial WWF star in the 1980s. He beat Bob Backlund for the WWF title, but only held it for a week.

Italian Stallion: Noted jobber in Mid-Atlantic and NWA territories during the late 1970s and early 1980s.

Ivan Koloff: This former WWF world champion feuded with Bruno Sammartino and was a talented wrestler, despite his short stature. He lives in North Carolina.

Ivan Putski: A powerful weightlifter who became a top WWF tag-team mainstay in the 1970s, he adopted a Polish strongman gimmick.

Ivory: A former women's champ for GLOW in the early 1980s, she bided her time and got a shot in WWF and won the women's title there. She is now a fitness guru.

J

Jack Brickhouse: Legendary sports broadcaster from Chicago who announced pro wrestling in that city during the 1950s and 1960s.

Jack Brisco: A multi-talented amateur and pro wrestler, he is one of the sport's few Native Americans. Respected in and out of the ring, he was a top NWA star in the 1970s, feuded with Harley Race and the Funks, and is a former world champion.

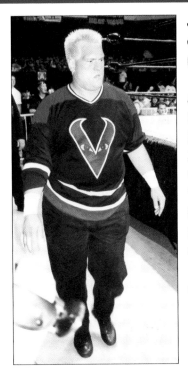

Jack Victory.

Jack Victory: Man of a million gimmicks, he was a Secret Serviceman, a bodyguard, a New Zealander, etc. He was best as Jack Victory and won the UWF tag title in the mid-1980s He was recently in ECW as Steve Corino's guide.

Jackie Fargo: Old-time Louisville and Memphis legend, he was part of the Fabulous Fargos.

Jackie Fulton: Younger brother of Bobby Fulton, he wrestled with his brother in the 1990s and the New Fantastics.

Jacques Rougeau: Canadian star who wrestled with his brother, Raymond, in the WWF, he later he went to single's ranks as the Mountie.

Jake Millimen: Lifetime jobber from the Midwest.

Jake Roberts: Became famous on the national level as the Snake and was a second-generation star who cut his teeth in Mid-South, Florida, and Memphis. He even traveled with a pet snake. He rarely won titles, though.

Jamie Dundee: Son of Bill Dundee, this small but talented wrestler wrestled with Wolfie D as PG-13 for more than five years and stays around the Memphis area.

Jay Strongbow: A consummate tag-team wrestler, he was at his peak in the 1970s and teamed with Billy White Wolf, Tony Garea, and Pedro Morales.

Jay Youngblood: Indian gimmicked star from the WWF during the 1970s.

Jeep Swenson: A Dallas tough man who feuded with Bruiser Brody in the World Class group.

Jeff Hardy: A North Carolina native who trained himself to wrestle, he gives all backyard wrestlers hope. With his brother Matt, he won WWF tag gold and got his break working for Jim Cornette in SMW during the mid-1990s.

Jeff Jarrett.

Jeff Jarrett: A second-generation star from Memphis, he started his career at a very young age and looked like a bean pole then, but eventually matured into a top U.S. star. He has won WWF I-C and tag titles and is a former WCW champ.

Jerry Brisco: Brother of Jack, this fine tactical wrestler is now a WWF road agent and runs a body shop in Florida. With his brother, he had classic matches with the Funks in the 1970s.

Jerry Flynn: A trained kick boxer from Florida, he got a break in WCW a few years ago and trained with Norman Smiley.

Jerry Jarrett: A better-than-average wrestler in the 1970s, he became a touted promoter in Memphis and was a one-time owner of USWA. He is the father of Jeff Jarrett.

Jerry Lawler: A true Renaissance man, he is an artist, disc jockey, politician, talk show host, color commentator, wrestler, and singer. Few have lived such a storied life. Known as "The King," Lawler is a quick-witted man who put Memphis wrestling on the map.

Jerry Lynn.

Jerry Lynn: Former ECW champ who was trained by Brad Rheingans, he is one of the best technical wrestlers today. He was Mr. J.L in WCW under the mask and had a classic feud with Rob Van Dam.

Jerry Morrow: Nicknamed "Champagne," he wrestled in Canada during the 1980s for Stampede.

Jesse Barr: Brother of Art Barr from a Portland family, he wrestled as Jimmy Jack Funk in WWF and other groups during the 1980s, although he's no relation to the Funks.

Jesse Ventura: Adopting his persona from Billy Graham, he became a powerful-looking man in the 1970s and 1880s and was nick-named "The Body." He was never a great wrestler, but was a wonderful talker. He has had roles in multiple Hollywood movies and is known worldwide as the wrestler turned Minnesota governor.

Jim Brunzell: This very skilled flyer in AWA teamed with Greg Gagne and used a Bruce Springsteen look in the ring during the 1980s. He was later one-half of the Killer Bees.

Jim Cornette: He began his career as a photojournalist and was a high-profile man-ager for nearly 20 years. He will always be associated with the Midnight Express, but has managed numerous champions. He is now content with training young stars in Kentucky and Indiana.

Jim Crockett: A one-time great promoter of the NWA, he dominated the Mid-Atlantic areas and sold his promotion to Ted Turner.

Jim Duggan: A four-decade veteran known for his brawls in the South, he was nick-named "Hacksaw" and became a comedy act in the WWF and WCW during the 1990s. He later returned to the ring after a bout with cancer.

Jim Londos: The first "Golden Greek," he claimed wrestling was real in his day (the 1940s).

Jim Neidhart: Trained under the Hart family in Calgary, he teamed with Bret Hart as the Hart Foundation and is a former tag champ. He was nicknamed "the Anvil" and is known for his trademark goatee.

Jim Ross: One of the best announcers of all time, he started his career with Bill Watts' Mid-South wrestling and moved on to WCW and then WWF. He has shown tremendous courage in his battles with a condition called Bells Palsy and is the voice of the WWF.

Jimmy Del Rey: Tennessee wrestler who teamed with Tom Pritchard as the Heavenly Bodies, he was also a SMW tag champ.

Jimmy Garvin: Brother of Ron Garvin, he was nicknamed "Handsome," has been to NWA and AWA, and was the fourth Freebird.

Jimmy Golden: Tennessee-based wrestler who had a WCW stint as Bunkhouse Buck, he was never far from Robert Fuller.

Jimmy Hart: Nicknamed "Mouth of the South," he was a famous manager from the 1980s who started in Memphis. He had a big-money feud with Jerry Lawler and was at the center of the Lawler-Andy Kaufman angle. He went to WWF and managed mul-tiple champi-ons, but his career slowed in WCW in later years. He is good friends with Hulk Hogan.

Jimmy Hart.

Jimmy Snuka: Very muscular in his heyday during the late 1970s and early 1980s, "The Superfly" used the top-rope leap to dazzle fans. He was a favorite of promoter Vince McMahon and teamed with Bruiser Brody in Japan. He is still active on the independent scene.

Jimmy "Superfly" Snuka.

Jimmy Valiant: Talented and blond rock-'n'-roll wrestler from the 1970s and 1980s, he is a favorite in the South and was nicknamed the "Boogie Woogie Man." He also teamed with brothers Johnny and Jerry.

JJ Dillon: Former manager of the Four Horsemen from NWA, he worked in the front offices of WWF and WCW recently.

Joe E. Legend: Canadian star who now wrestles as Just Joe in WWF.

Joel Gertner: One-time fan turned announcer turned manager, he has been with ECW since its inception and is known for his double entendres during interviews.

Jody Hamilton: After a career as the Assassin, he became a scout for WCW and allegedly discovered Kevin Nash at a bar.

Joe Malenko: His real name is Jody and he's the brother of Dean from WWF. A master of submission holds, he toured often in Japan in the late 1980s.

Joey Abs: A WWF trainee looking for an identity, he now wrestles with Memphis Power Pro.

Joey Mathews: A cruiserweight tag-team wrestler with Christian York, he wrestles on the East Coast.

John Studd: A protégé of Killer Kowalski, together they won WWF tag titles as the Executioners. He was 6-8, 350 pounds, and feuded with Andre the Giant.

John Tolos: A Greek wrestler from Los Angeles during the 1960s and 1970s, he was noted for his blood-bath feuds with Fred Blassie and the Destroyer. He also managed as the Coach for a short time in the WWF.

Johnny Ace: Brother of Road Warrior Animal, he was part of Dynamic Dudes in WCW and has been in Japan through the 1990s. He's now a scriptwriter in WCW.

Johnny Rodz: A respected WWF jobber from the 1970s, he is now a trainer in New York.

Johnny Smith: A Canadian star in the 1980s, he has had many tours of Calgary and Japan.

Johnny Valentine: Known for a bullying ring style in the 1960s, he was a top draw during that time and spent his entire career as a rulebreaker. He suffered many ailments from a 1970s plane wreck.

Jonnie Stewart: Was a prelim wrestler in the Midwest in the early 1990s and was part of the last AWA group. He once tried out for a managing spot in WWF.

Jos LeDuc: A star from the 1960s to 1980s, he played the role of a Canadian lumberjack and was in many blood baths. He once even cut his arm on live TV with an axe.

Jose Gonzales: Wrestled under a mask as the Invader in Puerto Rico and was acquitted in 1988 in the murder of Bruiser Brody. He spent his career in the World Wrestling Council.

Jumbo Tsuruta: One of Japan's revered athletes before his death in 1999 from cancer, he defeated Nick Bockwinkel for the AWA title and was a great tag-team wrestler.

Junkyard Dog: Sylvester Ritter was a big star in the Mid-South for Bill Watts in the early 1980s. This African-American wrestler had a loyal following in Louisiana and became a national star in the WWF.

Jushin Liger: A masked Japanese star who was a WCW cruiser-weight champ, he had some of the best matches in the world in the mid-1990s.

Justin Credible: A former ECW champ now in WWF teaming with X-Pac, he has been to Memphis as well. he is a small but talented worker.

Justin Credible wears the shirt of his favorite wrestler.

Juventud Guerrera: This Mexican superstar is as aerial as a wrestler can be. A former WCW cruiser champ, he once mimicked the Rock on WCW television.

K

Kabuki: One of manager Gary Hart's assassins in the 1970s in Florida, he blew green mist at his opponents.

Kane: Glenn Osborne has been an underrated performer in WWF. He failed as Isaac Yankem, but went to the minors to learn his craft. As Kane, he is a WWF mainstay and once held the world title. He is also the story-line brother of Undertaker and held a tag title with Mankind.

Kanyon: Chris Kanyon is an innovator of moves and also works in Hollywood: He wrote wrestling choreography for Jesse Ventura's life-story TV special on NBC. He buddies around with Diamond Dallas Page and started as a masked wrestler.

Karl Gotch: A noted shooter who was part of the Legionnaire team with Rene Goulet in the early 1970s, he is considered a legend in Japan and remains a proponent of real wrestling.

Karl Gotch, left, and Lou Thesz at an autograph session in Japan.

Kat: Her real name is Stacy Carter. She was a gal pal of Jerry Lawler and he brought her into wrestling, and the two are now married. She was in WWF for several years, but was fired. She was also once the manager of Chyna.

Kato Kung Lee: This high flyer was a main-event star in Mexico and Japan in the 1970s.

Kimala: He weighed more than 350 pounds when he adopted the Ugandan Warrior gimmick and was known for slapping his bulbous belly. He was a main-event monster in Memphis, World Class, and the WWF.

Kaz Hayashi: This WCW cruiserweight is very competent, but a small performer. He is part of the Yung Dragons.

Kelly Kiniski: A second-generation star from AWA during the early 1980s.

Ken Patera: Once a competitive weightlifter who appeared in strongman contests, he won the WWF I-C title and was in AWA for many years.

Kendall Windham: Brother of Barry, he was too skinny to be a credible champion, but he won titles in the Florida group and later went to NWA.

Kendo Nagasaki: Japanese nemesis of Dusty Rhodes, he wrestled a lot in Florida and Dallas during the 1980s.

Ken Shamrock: Prior to his days in ultimate fighting, Vince Torelli was a pro wrestler in the Carolinas and toured Japan and Florida as well. His shoot fighting stardom led him to the big money of the WWF and at one point he seemed poised for superstardom and won the Intercontinental title. He has since returned to ultimate fights.

Ken Timbs: Georgia and Alabama lightweight from the 1970s and 1980s.

Kenny Jay: The Sodbuster was a legendary jobber in the Midwest in the 1960s and 1970s and holds victories over Harley Race and Bobby Heenan.

Kerry Von Erich: The most successful of the Von Erich (Adkisson) boys, he once held the NWA title and was a former WWF I-C

champ. He lost his lower leg in a motorcycle crash and continued to wrestle despite the injury. He was a very friendly man, but committed suicide while in the depths of depression.

Kevin Kelly: Kevin Wacholz was also known as Mr. Magnificent and wrestled in the AWA and World Class. He went to the WWF and performed as Nailz.

Kevin Nash: Found at a Georgia cannery and introduced to wrestling, he started his career as the Master Blaster and later as Oz. He went to WWF as Diesel, a bodyguard, and eventually won the world title. He left for WCW, formed the Outsiders with Scott Hall, was at the center of the New World Order, and was a huge star of the late 1990s. He also played college hoops at Tennessee.

Kevin Sullivan: This muscular Boston native began wrestling in the 1970s and became a fan favorite in Georgia in the early 1980s. He adopted a demonic style while in Florida and is the brainchild of such gimmicks as the Dungeon of Doom. He was once married to Nancy Sullivan, better known as the valet, Woman.

Kevin Sullivan and Mike Graham in a barbed-wire match.

Kevin Von Erich: The last remaining Von Erich son, he was a champion in World Class, wrestled barefoot, and was famous for his feud with the Freebirds. He left the wrestling business some time ago.

Kid Kash.

Kid Kash: This former ECW TV champ wrestled in the Southeast for many years before getting a break. He is a spectacular high flyer and his feud with EZ Money is fantastic.

Kid Romeo: A WCW cruiser-weight wrestler.

Killer Brooks: King of Texas ring wars in the 1970s, he was a holder of the coveted Texas Brass Knuckles title.

Killer Karl Kox: Famed Texas Brass Knuckles contender of the 1960s, he was also a main-event wrestler in California.

Killer Khan: A wild-eyed wrestler from Asia who challenged Hulk Hogan for the WWF title in the mid-1980s, he was managed by Mr. Fuji.

Killer Kowalski, right, and Blackjack Lanza share a moment.

Killer Kowalski: One of the biggest men of the 1950s and master of the Claw hold, he allegedly bit off the ear of wrestler Yukon Eric in a match. He settled in the WWF in the 1970s and was an all-time great villain.

King Curtis: A hardcore legend of the 1950s through 1970s, he won major titles in Hawaii, Australia, and WWF. An odd-looking character with his scars and bald head, he once teamed with Ripper Collins.

King Kong Bundy: Quite speedy even at 400 pounds, to give foes a fair chance he allowed opponents to get a five-count from the referee, rather than the traditional three-count. He toured virtually every major territory in the 1980s and starred in WWF rings for five-plus years. He was challenged for the world title at Wrestlemania II.

King Mabel: This former 1995 King of the Ring winner also wrestled as Viscera.

Kinji Shibuya: This barefooted iron man was a heel and used U.S. conflicts with Japan as a story-line motivator. He was well known in AWA and California.

Koko B. Ware.

Koko B. Ware: Once part of the PYT's tag team, he was brought to WWF with painted hair like a parrot. He made a nice living, but was not a main-event star.

Konnan: WCW Filthy Animals leader and once AAA champ in Mexico, he was once tapped to be Max Moon in WWF, but he turned down the idea.

Kronus: An East Coast wrestler from ECW who once teamed with Saturn, he is now in XPW.

Krusher Kowalski: Stan Kowalski toured Canada and won numerous belts in the 1950s and often teamed with Tiny Mills, a.k.a. Big K.

Kurt Angle: Former Olympic champion turned pro wrestler, he is one of the fastest-improving wrestlers ever. In his first year in wrestling, he won three different titles, including the world belt. He is also as funny on the mike as he is skilled in the ring. He started in Memphis Power Pro.

Kwee Wee: WCW cruiserweight from the Power Plant.

L

La Parka: Mexican star with a flair for throwing chairs.

La Parka, with Disco Inferno.

Lance Russell: This classy and legendary Memphis announcer has been going strong since the 1960s and is the voice of Memphis wrestling.

Lance Storm.

Lance Storm: A Canadian star who is a nutritional junkie, this former ECW tag champion teamed with Chris Jericho in SMW. He won the WCW U.S. title recently and leads Team Canada in WCW.

Larry Cameron: African-American strongman and former Stampede champ, he was a part-time member of WCW's Doom. He died while on tour in Germany.

Larry Hennig: Began his career as Verne Gagne's protégé in the 1960s and eventually turned on his mentor. He partnered with Harley Race and they formed a famous tag team from the 1960s. He was also known as "Pretty Boy" and is the father of Curt Hennig.

Larry Hennig, with his son Curt.

Larry Sharpe: His ring career was marred by numerous injuries, but he went on to train Bam Bam Bigelow at his Monster Factory camp.

Larry Simon: Was known as Professor Boris Malenko and had an illustrious career from the 1950s to the 1970s. He invented the Russian Chain match and trained the Malenko boys, as well as X-Pac and Norm Smiley.

Larry Zbyszko: As Larry Whistler, few fans appreciated him. He was "adopted" by Bruno Sammartino and his career took off, but he eventually feuded with Bruno and they had a match at Shea Stadium before 35,000 spectators. He called himself the "Living Legend" and was a multi-promotion champion.

Lash LeRoux: Louisiana-born, he climbed the ladder in WCW and went from jobber to cruiserweight champ. He has brilliant red hair.

Lelani Kai: Female wrestler who formed the Glamour Girls in the WWF during the 1980s.

Len Montana: As the Zebra Kid, he won numerous titles in the 1950s and will forever be known as Luca Brazzi from the film "The Godfather."

Lenny Lane: Independent star who reached stardom in WCW with teammate Lodi.

Leo Nomellini: Former college football star who held the record for most consecutive stars in the NFL— he never missed a game in 14 seasons. He wrestled in the 1950s and 1960s and often was a troubleshooting referee. He is also an NFL Hall of Fame member.

Les Thatcher: A top NWA junior heavyweight in the 1960s and 1970s, he now trains wrestlers in the Ohio region.

Lex Luger: A Florida native who was pegged to be the next superstar, he was popular indeed, but failed to live up to the hype. A former WCW champ, he has been a high-profile employee for 10 years and went to WWF, but did not win any title.

Lex Luger.

Lita: Once was Miss Congeniality in ECW and trained by the Hardy Boys. She once managed Essa Rios and is a former WWF women's champ. She could be a break-out star and is the real-life girlfriend of Matt Hardy.

Little Guido: An ECW shooter who is well-conditioned, he is part of Full Blooded Italians team with Tracy Smothers and Tommy Rich, and a former tag champ.

Lord James Blears: Distinguished Brit who announced and promoted in Hawaii in the 1960s and 1970s.

Lord Oliver Humperdink: Red Sutton found his niche as a manager in Florida and the WWF and had many feuds with Dusty Rhodes.

Lord Oliver Humperdink.

Lord Steven Regal: Well-schooled English wrestler who has had success in WCW and now WWF. He is known for witty facial expressions.

Lord Steven Regal.

Lou Albano: Held the WWF tag title in the late 1950s with Tony Altimore and later became a manager. The captain managed numerous tag champs including the Samoans.

Lou Thesz: Had an unbelievable win record from the 1940s to 1970s, and even wrestled a match in the 1990s. He is a multi-time NWA champion and one of the legends.

Luke Graham: Wacky character of the 1950s and 1960s in the WWF and also the Southwest area.

Luna Vachon: A member of the Vachon family, she began wrestling more than 10 years ago and is married to Gangrel.

Luther Lindsay: One of the only African-American shooters, he was a favorite of Stu Hart's, played Canadian football, and was a star from the 1950s to 1960s.

Madusa: This Minnesota beauty was once a valet in the AWA and trained to be a wrestler and made big money in Japan; she even recorded an album there. She has won the WWF and WCW women's titles and even the WCW cruiserweight title. She now races monster trucks.

Mae Young: A four-decade female wrestler, she is good friends with Fabulous Moolah and showed up in the WWF in 1999, providing many laughs.

Magnum T.A.: Terry Allen was a superstar in the NWA in the early 1980s, had a good look, and was adept in the ring. He held the U.S. title and feuded with Tully Blanchard. A protégé of Dusty Rhodes, he suffered partial paralysis in a car accident which ended his bright career.

Magnum Tokyo: Has potential to be the next major star in Japan and is the object of desire with females. He was in WCW in the late 1990s and is now part of Toryumon group.

Mando Guerrero: The shortest member of the Guerrero family, he was never far from his brothers, loved to fly high, and was mainly a star in the 1980s.

Manny Fernandez: A Southwest star who wrestled in Texas and Florida, he was often a good guy, but later turned heel. He teamed with Rick Rude and won NWA tag belts. His finisher was the Flying Burrito.

Marc Mero: As Johnny B. Badd, he was a novelty act in WCW in the early 1990s. He moved on to WWF, but did not live up to the hype. He is the husband of Sable and a former amateur boxer.

Mark Ash: "Mean Mark" promoted in Georgia and on the Gulf Coast, and is a longtime maker of wrestling boots.

Mark Henry: An agile big man who was an Olympic weightlifter in 1996, he is an underrated talent who was demoted to the minor leagues when his WWF career slowed.

Mark Jindrak: Partner of Sean O'Hare in WCW, he is very agile for his size.

Mark Lewin: An upstate New York strongman who toured New Zealand, England, Japan, Canada, and the U.S. from the 1960s to 1980s, he feuded with the Sheik in Detroit. His brothers, Ted and Don, also wrestled.

Mark Rocco: British star who wrestled as Rollerball Rocco in the early 1980s.

Marty Janetty: As half of the Midnight Rockers with Shawn Michaels, they became a super team in the 1990s and won tag belts in AWA and WWF. He later moved to singles wrestling, but never duplicated his tag-team success.

Matt Borne: Son of Tough Tony, a Portland-area star, Borne got a break as Big Josh in WCW and as Doink in the WWF.

Matt Hardy: Real-life brother of Jeff Hardy, he wrestled for New Dimension Wrestling before going to WWF. He has a real-life relationship with Lita.

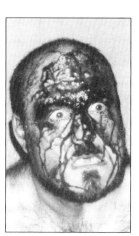

Mad Dog Vachon, after a match with The Crusher.

Maurice "Mad Dog" Vachon: A 1948 Olympic wrestler, he was a main-event star from the 1940s to 1980s and knew two styles in the ring: fast and faster. He and his brother, Butcher Vachon, won many tag titles and he is also a former AWA champ. Born in Montreal, Canada, he now lives in Omaha, Nebraska.

Michael Hayes: One of the greatest interviews in wrestling history, he could make you laugh, cry, and scream all in one interview. Famed leader of the Fabulous Freebirds, he was a main-event star wherever he went through the 1980s. He now works with WWF as an announcer.

"Pretty boy" Michael Hayes.

Mick Foley: A three-time WWF champion, Foley had many alter egos: Dude Love, Cactus Jack, and the immensely popular Mankind. Cactus Jack was the most violent of his characters. Foley tore up his body in Japan in many barbed wire and exploding ring matches and beat the odds to win those three championships. Foley wrote a best-selling book and eventually retired from wrestling, due to multiple injuries and concussions.

Mideon: A former WWF mid-card wrestler, he was also formerly in WCW.

Mike Awesome: A highly unusual wrestler, he is huge but moves like a cruiserweight. He worked for almost 10 years in Japan and wrestled as the Gladiator for FMW and even painted his face. He has been in some bloody wars and is a former ECW champ. He eventually moved on to WCW and is now part of Team Canada.

Mike Mazurky: Called Iron Mike in his wrestling days, he used his Hollywood connections to get himself and fellow wrestlers of the 1950s and 1960s coveted roles in film and on TV.

Mike Modest: A San Francisco technician trying to break into WWF or WCW, he is in the movie, "Beyond the Mat."

Mike Rapada: a.k.a. the Colorado Kid, he has been an NWA regional champion in the late 1990s and once held the USWA world title.

Mike Rotunda: Syracuse star who had a long and productive ring career, he spent many years in Japan and was a star in Florida and later the NWA. He won many titles and was a member of the Varsity Club with Steve Williams and Rick Steiner. He was also called IRS in the WWF and teamed with Barry Windham in the 1980s.

Mike Sanders: Power Plant grad with a gift for gab, he is leader of Natural Born Thrillers in WCW.

Mike Sanders.

Mike Von Erich: One of the Von Erich sons, he committed suicide 1987.

Mil Mascaras: Aaron Rodriguez was a body builder chosen by an entertainment firm to play Mil in Mexican movies and became an international draw in the 1970s. He often was used as a special attraction in the U.S. The man of a thousand masks is said to have never worn the same mask twice.

Missing Link: Got into wrestling late in life and last wrestled in his 40s. He was a strange person and painted his face green and blue, and his hair was cut like a maniac's 'do. He was a Mid-South, World Class, and WWF heel.

Missy Hyatt: Popular eye candy for World Class, UWF, and WCW in the 1980s and 1990s.

Mitch Snow: A Central States undersized but acrobatic jobber, he wrestled in the AWA.

Mitsuhara Misawa: Was the second Tiger Mask in Japan and for much of the 1990s, he was considered the best pro wrestler in the world. He was a champ of All-Japan and defected from that group and started his own promotion in 2000.

Mongolian Stomper: Archie Gouldie is one of the best conditioned athletes of any era and wrestled in Canada and toured the U.S. from the 1960s to 1980s.

Moose Cholok: One of the first 300-pound men seen on Chicago wrestling in the early 1960s, he often wore amateur headgear to the ring.

Mr. Fuji: Manager from the WWF, he was once a wrestler and even held the WWF tag title with Mr. Saito. He always carried a cane and spoke in broken English.

Mr. Hughes: A Central States wrestler who was big and athletic, he wrestled as the Big Cat and worked in the ring with sunglasses on. He was in WCW and WWF until recently.

Mr. Perfect Curt Hennig: He considered himself to be the perfect athlete while in the WWF in the 1990s. The son of Larry Hennig, he is a former AWA champ and won the WWF Intercontinental title. Plagued by injuries of late, he recently wrestled Dennis Rodman in Australia.

Mr. Pogo: This wild, face-painted Japanese star loves to cut opponents open with assorted metal objects and even used a power drill and chainsaw to "cut open" a foe. He feuded with Onita and Tarzan Goto.

Mr. Perfect Curt Hennig.

Mr. Saito: Classic Japanese star who won the AWA title in the early 1990s. He was a major player in Japan for many years and also teamed with Jesse Ventura in the early 1980s.

Mr. Wrestling II: A Georgia star from the 70s, this masked man was a local favorite for many years. His plain white mask, trunks, and boots were his trademarks.

New Jack: ECW risk-taker and part of the Gangstas' tag team, he enjoys using foreign objects and has even used stop signs, computer keyboards, and cheese graters to bash opponents with.

N

Nasty Boys: Brian Knobbs and Jerry Saggs made up this strange duo and won titles in the AWA, WWF, and WCW. Knobbs is now a single's wrestler as Saggs has retired due to injury.

Nelson Royal: A top NWA light heavyweight from the 1960s and 1970s, he claims to have invented the Bunkhouse Stampede match.

Nick Bockwinkel: One of the more technically sound performers of any era, he was a former AWA champ in the 1980s. He was comfortable in teams with Ray Stevens, Mr. Saito, and Bobby Heenan, and was an eloquent speaker in interviews.

Nick Kiniski : Son of Gene, he was an AWA prelim wrestler in the 1980s and wrestled in Portland as well.

Nikolai Volkoff: The first Volkoff was a small Russian man from the 1950s; the newer Nick was of European descent and loved to roughhouse his foes. He was a tag-team wrestler in WWF and a star from the 1960s to 1980s. He also insisted on singing the Russian national anthem before his matches.

Nicole Bass: Muscular woman who tried to find a niche as a bodyguard in the Chyna mold, she never caught on. She was in ECW and later WWF.

Nikita Koloff: He wrestled as a Russian but was from the Midwest and his first match ever was with Ric Flair in front of a capacity crowd. He was very stiff in the ring but knew how to be a tremendous heel. He won tag titles and singles titles and teamed with "uncle" Ivan Koloff, as well as Dusty Rhodes as the Super Powers in the 1980s.

Nord the Barbarian: After several years as a prelim bum, he adopted the Barbarian gimmick and was asked by Bruiser Brody to carry on his legacy. He went to Mid South and AWA, became the Berserker in the WWF in the early 1990s, and retired from injuries.

Nova: This East Coast wrestler has been in ECW for five years and is an innovator of moves.

Norman Smiley.

Norman Smiley: a.k.a. "Black Magic" and a noted shooter with Virgin Island ties, he traveled to Japan and Mexico before finding a spot with WCW. He trained with the Malenko family and is a very tough man in real life.

Owen Hart: One of the special performers of the modern era who died tragically performing a stunt in 1998, he was a high flyer in Canada and Japan and teamed with his brother Bruce and held Calgary title. He feuded with Makhan Singh, wrestled as Blue Blazer for many years, was a WWF tag champ with Jeff Jarret, and won the I-C title as well. He leaves a spectacular legacy.

Ox Baker: One of the most menacing forces to ever get in the ring, he is a veteran from the 1950s to 1970s. He is featured in the movie, "Escape from New York," and was well known in Midwest.

O

Ole Anderson: Along with "brother" Gene, he made up one half of the Minnesota Wrecking Crew and wreaked havoc in NWA and Mid-Atlantic in the 1970s. A rugged performer who brought an air of believability, he later adopted Arn Anderson into the fold and was also a writer for WCW.

One Man Gang: A 350-pound brawler who hails from Chicago and has been to many territories, he held the UWF title and wrestled as Akeem. He won the WWF tag title and also had a fun gimmick.

Otto Wanz: A legend in Germany who wrestled in the AWA in the 1970s, he won the AWA title from Nick Bockwinkel and once tore a phone book in half with his hands. He is now a promoter in his native land.

Outback Jack: A failed gimmick used in the WWF in the early 1980s, he came in with a bang, but left with a whimper.

P

Pampero Firpo: A wild-haired maniac from the 1960s, he claimed he was from South America and kept foreign objects in his mop hairdo.

Pat O'Connor: A famed NWA champion from New Zealand, his biggest impact was made in the 1950s and 1960s. He was a shooter-type wrestler and always played the good guy. He often gave 45- to 60-minute performances and had controversial battles with Lou Thesz.

Pat Patterson: A top draw in San Francisco in the 1960s, this single's star and also partner of Ray Stevens ventured to the WWF and had a classic boot-camp match with Sgt. Slaughter. He had a brief run as a I-C title holder and was a backstage employee in WWF.

Pat Tanaka: Short, karate expert from the 1980s and early 1990s, he wrestled barefoot. He teamed with Paul Diamond in AWA and was Akio Sato's partner in WWF as Orient Express.

Paul Bearer: Formerly Percy Pringle and the Dallas manager of Rick Rude, he was a great heel in his day. Yes, he is a former funeral-parlor worker, and also managed Undertaker, Kane, and Mankind in WWF.

Paul Boesch: Longtime Houston promoter who retired in the 1980s, he wrestled briefly in the 1940s and 1950s.

Paul Diamond: A former pro soccer player from Florida, he played Max Moon in WWF and won numerous tag titles with Pat Tanaka.

Paul E. Dangerously: A former manager turned promoter and announcer, he was an ECW promoter who has a penchant for the Extreme. As a manager, he guided the Original Midnight Express to gold and was seen in Memphis, NWA, and AWA. He was brilliant at dreaming up wrestler's gimmicks and is now a commentator for WWF.

Paul Ellering: Former weightlifting champion and prelim wrestler who turned to managing, he guided the Road Warriors to stardom. He also took part in sled-dog races in Alaska.

Paul Neu: He wrestled as P.N. News in WCW and rapped in the ring. He is now in Germany wrestling and energizing crowds.

Paul Orndorf: A legit tough man with a football background, he toured around the world, but found a home in the WWF and his feud with Hulk Hogan is a classic. He went to WCW and now heads the WCW training center.

Paul Roma: This well-sculpted wrestler from the 1980s was mostly a prelim worker and teamed with Hercules and Paul Orndorff.

Pedro Martinez: Was popular in the Cleveland and Pittsburgh regions through the 1960s.

Pedro Morales: The first major Puerto Rican star to become champion of a major U.S. group, this top 1970s star won WWF world, I-C and tag titles and had a remarkable 75-minute draw with Bruno Sammartino at Shea Stadium.

Pete Gas: Childhood friend of Shane McMahon, he was brought to WWF as part of the Greenwich Posse and never trained to be a wrestler. He was a whipping boy in WWF and is now in Memphis.

Pez Whatley: This Texas and Mid-South African-American mainly worked as a heel and won regional titles in the 1980s.

Phil Hickerson: This large Memphis wrestler found a home in the USWA during the late 1980s/early 1990s. He had feud with Eric Embry over USWA ownership, and even wrestled as an Asian named P.Y. Chu Hi.

Pitbulls: Muscled tag team from the East Coast who were in ECW before their shot at stardom was over.

Precious: 1980s valet of husband Jimmy Garvin...sprayed the ring with disinfectant prior to Garvin's arrival...was source of mayhem while in Dallas and in the NWA.

Prime Time Elix Skipper: African-American cruiserweight who teams with Lance Storm, is one of WCW's few young prospects, and has tremendous charisma.

Prince Albert: Called Baldo in Memphis, the pierced Albert teamed with Droz briefly in WWF. He is a very big man, but lacks true identity to be a star.

Prince Iukea: Polynesian wrestler from WCW, he also used the name Artist and was once a cruiserweight champ.

Psicosis: Mexican star who got a break in ECW and later WCW, he was forced to unmask along with other Latino wrestlers. He loves to fly.

Public Enemy: Rocco Rock and Johnny Grunge make up this odd duo and bounce around the ring like ping pong balls. Former ECW tag champs, they love breaking tables and were in WCW briefly.

R

Rey Mysterio Jr.: Second-generation star from San Diego by way of Tijuana, he was a spectacular junior heavyweight in his prime and has been with WCW since 1996.

Rey Mysterio Jr. meets and greets.

Randy Savage: This highly recognizable wrestler of the 1980s and 1990s has won both WCW and WWF titles. Nicknamed "Macho Man," his flamboyant costumes and trademark voice make him a favorite of many.

Macho Man Randy Savage.

Ranger Ross: An early 1990s gimmick wrestler from WCW, he toiled in prelims before leaving wrestling.

Ray Candy: Large Florida wrestler who made up one-half of the Zambuie Express in the early 1980s with Leroy Brown, he once wrestled in the Crockett Cup.

Ray Rougeau: French-Canadian brother of Jacques, he is now a successful promoter in Montreal.

Rhino: An ECW school grad who reminds some of Tazz, he enjoys plowing opponents through tables and his feud with Sandman was censored on TV due to its violent nature.

Rhino.

Ric Flair: He has held a world title more times than anyone (14) in history and is a legend in North Carolina, where he considered running for governor. He has mainly wrestled in the NWA, but had a tour of the WWF and won that title twice. He has had notable feuds with Hulk Hogan, Sting, Roddy Piper, Dusty Rhodes, and Harley Race, and is one of the all-time greats.

Ricky Santana: A Latino star who wrestles in Puerto Rico, he had tours of the U.S. during the 1980s for NWA.

Ricky Steamboat: A superb technician, he held the NWA title and wrestled a 60-minute draw with Ric Flair. He has also won the WWF I-C title, and few have been better pure wrestlers than Steamboat.

Ricky Steamboat, right, goes nose to nose with Roddy Piper.

Rikishi: One of many Samoan wrestlers in WWF, he was part of the Samoan Swat Team and Headshrinkers. He had several gimmicks before settling with Rikishi and uses his posterior anatomy to degrade opponents.

Rikishi, in his previous days as "Fatu."

Rip Rogers: A highly conditioned prelim star from the 1980s, he is mainly a Southeast face and works for OVW as a trainer.

Road Dogg: Brian James created this totally unique character in 1997 and tore the house down with his trademark quotes. He toiled in Memphis for years before catching a break with WWF and won the tag title with Billy Gunn. He was once Jeff Jarrett's lackey.

Robert Fuller: This Tennessee "Studd" is from a family of wrestlers, worked mainly in the South, and was Col. Robert Parker in WCW.

Robert Gibson: One-half of the Rock & Roll Express, he was less charismatic than his partner Ricky Morton, but was a talented wrestler.

Rock: Dwayne Johnson is a star for the New Millennium. A second-generation star, he has been every major champion in WWF and is truly the WWF's franchise player. His feuds with Mick Foley and Steve Austin show his finest work. He has now crossed over into film.

Rocky Johnson: Father of the Rock, Rocky was a star in the 1970s for the WWF and held the WWF tag title with Tony Atlas.

The Rock continues the wrestling tradition started by his father Rocky Johnson. In the photo above, The Rock, far right, poses with his father, mother, and wife Dani. In the bottom photo, Rocky Johnson is bloodied during a match with the Stomper, but managed to keep his title.

Rod Price: A former football player with the San Diego Chargers, he is very big and wrestled in California and Texas. He was also in ECW in the late 1990s.

Rowdy Roddy Piper adjusts to life as a Hollywood actor.

Roddy Piper: The Rowdy One claims he was a homeless 14-year-old when he thought about getting into wrestling and he turned pro at age 16. Piper became one of wrestling's biggest personalities in the 1980s and later turned to film. For many years, he was the No. 1 foe in the WWF and his feuds with Ric Flair and Mr. T are among his most significant. He is also a former U.S. title holder.

Rodney: Partner of Pete Gas in WWF, he got beat from pillar to post by main stars and is now called "Rodrageous" in Memphis.

Ron Simmons: Now called Farooq in the WWF, Simmons was an All-American football star at Florida State and is the first African American to hold the NWA world title. He began his career in Florida, but quickly moved to NWA/WCW and held tag belts with Butch Reed. He has now found a home in WWF with Bradshaw.

Ronnie Garvin: A former NWA champ nicknamed "Hands of Stone," his finisher was the knockout punch. He wrestled in WWF as "Rugged" Ron and has been a player since the 1970s. He retired in the mid-1990s after a final run in SMW.

Russ Francis: Brother of Ed who was a Hawaii-based promoter, Russ was an All-Pro receiver in the NFL and did well in wrestling through the 1970s.

S

Sable: Wife of Marc Mero, she never wanted to get into wrestling, but became a major player in WWF with her good looks and even had two pictorials in *Playboy*. She eventually left wrestling, claiming sexual harassment, but she lost her lawsuit and moved on to acting.

Sabu: Terry Brunk, the nephew of Sheik Ed Farhat, is a pioneering table breaker from Detroit and his wild style found him at home in ECW and Japan's FMW. Rob Van Dam was a dynamic partner of his once. Injuries and wear-and-tear have slowed his efforts of late.

Sailor Art Thomas: One of the few men to fight stereotyping in wrestling in the 1960s, he was a main-event star.

Sailor Art Thomas.

Sal E. Graziano: Nearly 400 pounds, he mostly manages, but is actually trained to wrestle.

Sam Houston: A second-generation wrestler, he is the brother of Jake Roberts and an NWA and Southeast mid-card wrestler. He held the Western States title and wrestles out of Texas.

Sam Muschnik: Legendary promoter in St. Louis, he made wrestling at The Chase Hotel famous.

Samoans: Whether Afa and Sika were on "Miami Vice" or cooking fish heads on wrestling TV, few were safe around them in the 1970s and 1980s and they won WWF tag titles.

Sandman: After cementing his legacy as an ECW icon, he ventured to WCW, but success was not found there and he went back to ECW. He works independents now and is famous for his brawling, bumps, and beer-chugging.

Satoru Sayama: A Japanese star who wrestled as the first Tiger Mask, he truly revolutionized the industry and wrestling today owes him a debt. He wrestled under the mask in the U.S. briefly in the early 1980s.

Saturn: WWF member of the Radicalz, he won the ECW tag title with John Kronus and took on a Marilyn Manson gimmick in WCW.

Savannah Jack: A former UWF TV title holder and former black belt and Gold Gloves champ, he retired due to heart trouble.

Scorpio: a.k.a. 2 Cold Scorpio, he has been to WWF, WCW, and ECW and is an acrobatic African-American.

Scott Hall: Started wrestling in the 1980s out of Florida and quickly moved to AWA, where he won a tag title with Curt Hennig. He was Gator Scott Hall in NWA in the late 1980s and underwent a total change in WWF, where he became Razor Ramon. He won the I-C title and dashed to WCW, where he became a huge star with Kevin Nash. He has been wrestling in Japan of late.

Scott Irwin: Along with his brother Bill, they made up the Longriders and Super Destroyers tag team in the 1970s and 1980s. Scott died in his 30s of a rare ailment, but Bill is still going strong and wrestled as the Goon in WWF.

Scott Norton: Former bouncer and arm wrestler turned ring wrestler, he had success in Japan, even winning the coveted IWGP title. He also had runs in WCW as part of the NOW and trained through the Gagne family in the AWA.

Scott Steiner: This former amateur at Michigan was once tabbed as heir apparent to Ric Flair. He was the first to use a huricanrana in the U.S. and won numerous tag titles with his brother Rick. He has held most major titles in WCW, including the world belt, and is totally unpredictable.

Scott Taylor: Wrestles as Scotty 2 Hotty in WWF and is famous for the "Worm." He often reminds fans of Eddie Gilbert and has been a teammate of Brian Christopher for several years.

Scotty 2 Hotty.

SD Jones: "Special Delivery" was a prelim favorite of the WWF and was squashed by King Kong Bundy once in a "record" eight seconds.

Sean O'Hare: A Power Plant grad and WCW tag-team champ, he could be a huge star one day.

Sgt. Slaughter: A big man who won many titles from the 1970s to 1990s, he wrestled mostly as a heel and also dabbled as a fan fave. His feuds with Pat Patterson and Hulk Hogan drew sell-out crowds and he held the WWF title briefly.

Shane Douglas: Most known for his role as the Franchise in ECW and WCW, he is a three-decade veteran and has a teaching degree, but insists on wrestling. He is also a great interview.

Shane Douglas puts the squeeze on Kristi Myst of XPW.

Shane Helms: Break-out cruiserweight in WCW, he has been partnered with Shannon Moore and Evan Karagis.

Shane McMahon: A fourth-generation wrestling genius, he will take over the reigns of WWF after his father, Vince Jr., retires. He is not a trained wrestler, but his forays into the ring have been nothing short of fantastic. He is afraid of nothing and once fell 70 feet off a stage in a match with Steve Blackman.

Shannon Moore: A Southern-based cruiser-weight, he started in NWA Wildside and is part of 3-Count tag team.

Shawn Michaels: A tremendous showman of the WWF, this former world champ was a tag-team wrestler before going singles and had a great feud with Bret Hart. He won tag titles in WWF and AWA with Marty Janetty in the late 1980s and retired early due to injury. He is a San Antonio native.

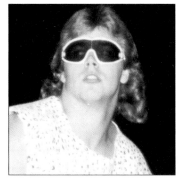

A young Shawn Michaels.

Shawn Stasiak: This second-generation star from WCW was called Meat in WWF and cut his teeth in Memphis. He was the love interest of Stacy Carter (The Kat).

Sheik Farhat: Wrestling's most-hated man in the 1960s and 1970s, he mainly wrestled out of Detroit and had a decade-long feud with Bobo Brazil. He used a fork to inflict pain on his opponents, has spilled copious amounts of blood, and is revered in Japan.

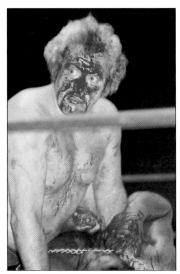

The Sheik in one of his classic matches with Bobo Brazil.

Sherri Martel: A wonderful female performer who rivaled some men in the ring, she is a former world champ, managed Shawn Michaels to WWF gold, and also guided Harlem Heat.

Sho Funaki: Japanese performer from WWF, he is a part-time trainer in a school run by Shawn Michaels.

Sid: His size and power have kept him on the minds of promoters around the U.S., but a major injury in 2001 put him on the shelf. A former WCW and WWF champ, he started his career as Lord Humongous.

Shima Nobunaga: This Japanese spark plug from Toryumon had a sting in the WCW cruiserweight division.

Simon Diamond: An East Coast independent wrestler, he won a coveted Delaware cruiserweight tournament, been with ECW, and is the real-life boyfriend of Dawn Marie.

Simpsons: A early 1980s team in Dallas, Steve and Scott were from South Africa and promoted to look like the Von Erichs.

Sky Hi Lee: He was nearly 7 feet tall and 300 pounds when he wrestled in the 1940s.

Slick: A manager in WWF during the mid-1980s, he called himself the Reverend and was guided Butch Reed. He eventually left wrestling altogether.

Sonny Onoo: Japanese liaison between WCW and New Japan group before he was fired, he has managed Ernest Miller and is pals with Eric Bischoff.

Spike Dudley: This former Wall Street stock broker had a passion for the ring and lived out a dream. He was not afraid to put his body in harm's way for the crowd's appreciation and found a home in ECW. He has since reunited with Dudley Boys in WWF.

No one stands taller in hardcore matches than Spike Dudley.

Spike Huber: Ex-construction worker turned wrestler in the 1980s, he hails from Indiana and worked in World Class, WWF, and WWA.

Stan Hansen: Noted as being one of the most rugged men ever, his Lariat clothesline often injured opponents for real. He is a star in Japan and won an AWA world title. A three-decade star, he recently retired.

Stan Lane: He and Steve Keirn made up the famous Fabulous Ones team in the 1980s and he later teamed with Bobby Eaton and is a former tag-team champ in NWA.

Stan Stasiak: Won the WWF title from Pedro Morales in 1973, is the father of Shawn, and was a large tough man.

Stanislaus Zbyszko: Born in Poland, he was a world champion from the 1920s, is said to be the first wrestler billed as the "8th Wonder of the World," and was the first wrestler to earn $1 million. He was also a World War II Allied translator.

Stephanie McMahon: She is "daddy's little girl" on TV and came out of nowhere to be a major star in WWF. She has been around wrestling her whole life and is the storyline wife of Triple H.

Steve Austin: He toiled in WCW for years and was plagued by injury, but then WWF took a chance on him in 1995 and he carved his own niche as Stone Cold and grew into the largest star wrestling has ever seen. His trademark 3:16 shirts have sold more than any other in wrestling and he has won the WWF title several times. His feud with Vince McMahon is one of the biggest money-grossing feuds of all-time.

Steve Blackman: This trained black belt was schooled by Bruce Hart in Canada and was poised for a WWF run, but he caught

Malaria. It took him more than two years to recover, but he has been a role player in WWF and has won a hardcore belt.

Steve Corino: This former ECW champ blends the styles of Bobby Heenan and a young Barry Windham, calls himself "Old School," and is a gifted talker.

Steve Doll: Well-traveled vet from the 1980s and 1990s, he has been to every territory and was one-half of Well Dunn in WWF with Rex King.

Steve Lombardi: Noted WWF jobber in the 1970s and 1980s, he was often called the "Brooklyn Brawler" and still works occasionally.

Steve McMichael: "Mongo" was a football player for the Bears and once married to Debra. He wrestled and announced for WCW in the mid-1990s, but has disappeared from wrestling.

Steve Strong: This well-muscled 1980s star, who wrestled in Calgary, California, and Hawaii, is said to be a talented painter.

Steve Keirn: Teamed as the Fabulous Ones with Stan Lane in the early 1980s, which was a hugely popular team of that era, this Florida native wrestled as Skinner in the WWF.

Steve Williams: A former amateur standout from Oklahoma and nicknamed "Dr. Death," he was a favorite of promoter Bill Watts. This terrific brawler is a former UWF champ.

Steve "Dr. Death" Williams.

Stevie Ray: Better known as Booker T's partner, he was part of the NWO for a time and one of the first African-American announcers in wrestling.

Sting: Steve Borden was discovered in California and broke in as the Ultimate Warrior's partner in the Blade Runners tag team. He later went his own way in UWF under the guidance of Eddie Gilbert and quickly rose up the ladder. He eventually had world-title shots, winning the NWA title, and has been a WCW icon.

Sting applies pressure on Ric Flair.

Strangler Ed Lewis: World champ of the 1920s and 1930s, he held the title at a time when declaring the rightful champ was a difficult task. He was infamous for squeezing the heads of his opponents in a blistering headlock. There was also an Evan Strangler Lewis in the late 1800s.

Super Crazy: A Mexican star from ECW who is a high flyer.

Swedish Angel: Tor Johnson also had a career in movies and was a star in the 1940s and 1950s.

T

Tajiri: He did not get recognized in his native Japan, so Yoshihiro Tajiri came to the

U.S. in the late 1990s and found a home in ECW. He brought with him several innovative moves and is a former tag champ.

Taka Michinoku: A Japanese star who lives for wrestling in the WWF, he was an independent wrestler overseas but could not get recognized by major companies. He is part of Kaientai in WWF.

Tazz.

Tammy Sytch: In the early 1990s, Sytch started in Jim Cornette's Smoky Mountain Wrestling group and caught on quickly as a manager. She also performed as Sunny in the WWF, has been in ECW at different times and got a huge break from the WWF to manage the Body Donnas, a team that included her boyfriend, Chris Candido.

Wrestling really is show biz, as Tammy Sytch helps her husband, Chris Candido, prepare for his match.

Tatanka: Chris Chavis got a chance as a Native American star in WWF during the early 1990s and won the I-C title there. The Native-American gimmick was given to him to capitalize on the movie, "Dances with Wolves."

Tatsumi Fujinami: This Japanese wrestler had success in the U.S. and was a star for many years with the New Japan group. He faced Ric Flair in a title-unification match in the early 1990s.

Tazz: A New York tough guy who has become a broadcaster for WWF, he is a former ECW champ and started as a face-painted Tasmanian Devil. He toiled in the independents because of size, but ECW took a chance on him and he became a star.

Ted Arcidi: Strongman from WWF during the early 1980s.

Ted DiBiase: A Mid-South second-generation star, he is a former Mid-South champ and was usually a fan fave. He went to WWF, became the Million Dollar Man, and totally lived the part: flying in private jets and riding in limos. He bought the WWF title from Andre the Giant and is now out of wrestling.

Teddy Long: This referee turned manager turned referee again was part of NWA for years. In his manager days, fans called him "Peanut Head". He now refs in WWF.

Terri Runnels: Former wife of Dustin Rhodes, she is former real-life secretary of Ted Turner and started in wrestling as a manager named Alexandra York. She guided a stable called the York Foundation and with her hubby, she went to WWF as a valet named Marlena. She and Rhodes eventually split up, though, and she now accompanies Saturn to the ring.

Terry Funk: A four-decade road-weary traveler who keeps going despite multiple injuries, he is former NWA champ and put many promotions on the map including ECW. He

Terry Funk.

is a true legend and his life is chronicled in the movie, "Beyond the Mat."

Terry Gordy: He began his career at 16 and is longtime partner of Michael Hayes. He wrestled in Japan for many years and fought through a coma in the 1990s to return to the ring.

The Maestro.

Terry Taylor.

Terry Taylor: A talented and gifted wrestler from the 1980s and 1990s, he appeared to be ready for world-champion status when his career went south. He was saddled with a Red-Rooster gimmick and is now a backstage writer.

Test: Andrew Martin debuted as a "roadie" for Motley Crue and quickly climbed the ranks. He was supposed to marry Stephanie McMahon, but she left him for Triple H. Test has toiled ever since, but should be a big player in the future.

Tex McKenzie: A star from the 1960s and 1970s who appeared in AWA, WWA, and IWA, he always wore a cowboy hat.

The Big Show: Once dubbed Andre the Giant Jr., Paul Wight suffers from the same ailment that Andre had and is massively large. He is a former WCW and WWF champ.

The Grappler: Real name Lynn Denton, he is formerly the Dirty White Boy, lives in Portland, and is semi-retired.

The Maestro: Once called Gorgeous George III, he played piano on his way to the ring in WCW.

The Spoiler: Masked heel from the 1970s found throughout the South.

The Wall: A large wrestler who is a WCW role player, he started as Alex Wright's bodyguard.

Thunderbolt Patterson: He fought WTBS in a discrimination suit and won, and was a star from the early 1980s.

Thunderfoot: Prelim masked star from the Georgia area during the 1980s.

Tiger Ali Singh: This Canadian-born wrestler from WWF has been used mainly as a manager.

Tiger Conway: Both Sr. and Jr. were wrestling stars, hail from Texas, and remain active business leaders.

Tiger Jeet Singh: King of bloodbaths in the 1960s and 1970s, he remains a cult hero in Japan.

Tim Horner: Talented light heavyweight from UWF and NWA in the early 1980s, he was Jim Cornette's partner in SMW.

Tito Santana: This talented ex-football player was a major star in the 1980s. He never had a bad match and won WWF tag and I-C titles.

Tojo Yamamoto: Former Tennessee wrestler who wreaked havoc from 1960s to 1980s, he sometimes teamed with Jerry Jarrett.

Tom Brandi: East Coast vet through the 1990s, he was in WWF briefly as Salvatore Sincere.

Tom Zenk: A former Mr. Minnesota who quit wrestling in the prime of his career, he is the former partner of Rick Martel and had many memorable bouts in Japan.

Tommy Dreamer: An ECW legend who has left body parts on the mat, he has had many terrific matches with Sandman and Raven.

Tommy Dreamer and a friend.

Tommy Gilbert: Father of Doug and the late Eddie Gilbert, he was a Southeast wrestler in the 1970s.

Tommy Rich: The youngest man to ever hold a NWA world title, he won it at age 17 in 1981 from Harley Race, and held the belt for a week. He has been around the world, but mostly wrestled in the Memphis area.

Tony Atlas: A former Mr. America contestant, he was a main-event star in NWA, WWF, and AWA in the 1970s and 1980s.

Tony Galento: Double-tough boxer who was often used as a special referee in the 1950s, he once fought Joe Louis for the heavyweight title.

Tony Garea: A longtime WWF employee, he was a top tag-team star of the 1970s.

Tony St. Clair: British technician from the 1980s and 1990s.

Tori: Former women's wrestler turned valet in WWF during the late 1990s, he managed X-Pac and Kane.

Torrie Wilson: Fitness model turned valet in WCW during the late 1990s, she managed Kidman and Shane Douglas.

Toru Tanaka: One of the many Japanese stars to appear in the U.S. as Odd Job, he often toured the West Coast in the 1970s.

Tracy Smothers: This friendly Southern-born wrestler was part of the Southern Boys tag team with Steve Armstrong and held the SMW title. He was part of the Full Blooded Italians team in ECW.

Trailer Park Trash: A Kentucky hardcore wrestler, he has been to OVW, Memphis, and Puerto Rico.

Trish Stratus: Former fitness model turned WWF valet, she has been the love interest of Vince McMahon on TV. She has managed Test and Albert as well.

Tugboat: A large wrestler who won the tag-team title in WWF during the early 1990s, he later went to WCW.

Tully Blanchard: An original member of the Four Horsemen, he is a second-generation star and won tag-team titles with Arn Anderson.

Ultimate Warrior: Jim Hellwig started his career as Sting's partner and moved to Dallas and became the Dingo Warrior. He left for WWF, where he changed his name to the Ultimate Warrior and unseated Hulk Hogan for the WWF title at Wrestlemania. He sued WWF over his namesake trademark, returned to WCW briefly, and lives in Arizona.

Ultimo Dragon: Sensational Japanese star who wears a mask, a shoulder injury ended his career in WCW and he now trains young-sters in Tokyo.

Undertaker: Mark Calloway brought life into a strange gimmick and wrestled as Mean Mark before heading to WWF in 1990, where he debuted at the Survivor Series. A three-time WWF champ, he has had many image changes over the years and is now the "American Badass." He continues wrestling, even through constant injuries.

Val Venis: Sean Morley had wrestled in Mexico extensively before signing with the WWF in 1997 and came to the group as an adult film star wanna-be. He is actually a multi-talented wrestler, has won the WWF I-C title, and is now a part of the Right to Censor group.

V

Van Hammer: This tall, energetic wrestler has not been consistent since starting with WCW in the early 1990s.

Vince McMahon: The greatest wrestling promoter of all-time, he is said to be a bil-lionaire, with holdings in several businesses. His family has a rich tradition in wrestling and he appears ready to pass that tradition to his son and daughter. He actually held his company's world title during a feud with Steve Austin and despite his age, McMahon is a well-conditioned fitness fanatic.

Vincent: Formerly Ted DiBiase's man ser-vant Virgil, he was part of the new NWO.

Keiji Mutoh hit the U.S. scene — like no other foreign star —

In the mid-1980s, a young Japanese sensation named Keiji Mutoh arrived in the U.S. like a firestorm. With him, he brought a unique, high-fly-ing style never scene before. Eventually, he made his way to the NWA and TBS wrestling. Like other Japanese stars before him (Kendo Nagasaki and Kabuki) Muto wore face paint. He called himself the Great Muta. One of his trademarks was spraying a green mist into the face of his opponents. But underneath the gimmickry was an outstanding tal-ent. His feud with Sting that culminated at the 1989 Great American Bash is still a popular video seller. When he returned to Japan, Mutoh was a major hit with his country and went on to become a headlin-er for New Japan, as himself and as the Great Muta. This New Japan Superstarz doll from the first series can be found for around $50 in the U.S.

W

Wahoo McDaniel: Legendary Native American star who played pro football, he was trained by the Funk family and was a star from the 1970s to 1980s in Mid-Atlantic, NWA, and AWA regions.

Wally Yamaguchi: Japanese referee and matchmaker, he was a manager of Kaientai in WWF.

Warlord: Terry Szopinski was a muscular tough man known for power moves and he teamed with Barbarian in the Powers of Pain group.

Wayne Munn: He had a short reign as world champion in the 1920s and died at age 35.

Wendy Richter: Female WWF star from the early 1980s, she dethroned Fabulous Moolah from her 30-year reign as women's champion. Richter was at the center of the Rock and Wrestling explosion of the early 1980s.

Whipper Watson: A two-time world champion from the 1940s.

Wilbur Snyder: A AWA star from the 1960s, he was a tag-team champ with Leo Nomellini.

Wild Bull Curry: Was a wild man in the ring said to have incited riots in the crowd. He was the brass-knuckles champ from the 1950s to 1970s and his son, Fred Curry, was also a wrestler.

William Muldoon: First-ever recognized wrestling champion, he was declared the champ in 1877 and was a Civil War soldier. Born in Ireland, he settled in New York and fought famed John L. Sullivan in the first wrestler vs. boxer match in 1880, but the match was stopped before a victor was decided. He ended up traveling with Sullivan and some wonder if they fixed their famous fight.

Woman: Nancy Sullivan was once married to Kevin Sullivan and followed him into wrestling. She managed dutifully in WCW and guided Doom and Rick Steiner. She ventured to ECW, but then went back to WCW, where she guided Chris Benoit. Her relationship with Benoit blossomed and the two recently had a child together.

X

X-Pac: Sean Waltman started his career at age 15 as 1-2-3 Kid and trained out of the Malenko school in Florida before moving to Minnesota. Waltman had a series of matches with Jerry Lynn and Ricky Rice that remain sought-after tapes. He combines styles from Japan, Calgary, and Mexico and has been in the middle of two revolutionary angles with the NWO and DX.

X-Pac in his days as the 1-2-3 Kid.

Y

Yokozuna: Rodney Anoia was once called "Kokina Maximus," a joke name that referred to his large backside. He once held the WWF title and was truly a sight to behold in the ring. He passed away in 2000 due to heart trouble.

Yousouf the Terrible Turk: A dock worker from France who was billed as a monster from Turkey in the early 1900s, he died in a shipwreck en route to Europe.

Yvon Robert: This French-Canadian star may have been the prototype for Ric Flair. He lived like a champion 24-7 and liked to wine and dine after the matches.

Z

Zeus: Tiny Lister is from Orange County, Calif. and played Hulk Hogan's nemesis in the "No Holds Barred" movie. He also wrestled some and had a feud with Hogan in WWF in the late 1980s.

Putting their stamp on the entire world

The WWF is everywhere. Candy bars, billboards, movies—and now stamps. In the late 1990s, the country of Liberia (known for its lackadaisical laws when it comes to putting commercial figures on stamps) introduced a line of stamps featuring Mankind, the Rock, and Steve Austin. Yes, they do hold value in Liberia. In the States, expect to find these gems for around $20. The stamps feature several different poses of the stars in the ring and in action. No word on whether the country has plans to introduce any further collections, so these may be a fan's only chance to find such an item. These were found at a stamp-collecting site on the Internet.